P9-ECN-339

WITHDRAWN
UTSA LIBRARIES

New Communication Technologies in Developing Countries

COMMUNICATION

A series of volumes edited by
Dolf Zillmann and **Jennings Bryant**

Zillmann/Bryant • Selective Exposure to Communication

Beville • Audience Ratings: Radio, Television, Cable, Revised Edition

Bryant/Zillmann • Perspectives on Media Effects

Goldstein • Reporting Science: The Case of Aggression

Ellis/Donohue • Contemporary Issues in Language and Discourse Processes

Winnet • Information and Behavior: Systems of Influence

Huesmann/Eron • Television and the Aggressive Child: A Cross-National Comparison

Gunter • Poor Reception: Misunderstanding and Forgetting Broadcast News

Olasky • Corporate Public Relations: A New Historical Perspective

Donohew/Sypher/Higgins • Communication, Social Cognition, and Affect

Van Dijk • News Analysis: Case Studies of International and National News in the Press

Van Dijk • News as Discourse

Wober • The Use and Abuse of Television: A Social Psychological Analysis of the Changing Screen

Kraus • Televised Presidential Debates and Public Policy

Masel Walters/Wilkins/Walters • Bad Tidings: Communication and Catastrophe

Salvaggio/Bryant • Media Use in the Information Age: Emerging Patterns of Adoption and Consumer Use

Salvaggio • The Information Society: Economic, Social, and Structural Issues

Olasky • The Press and Abortion, 1838–1988

Botan/Hazleton • Public Relations Theory

Zillmann/Bryant • Pornography: Research Advances and Policy Considerations

Becker/Schoenbach • Audience Responses to Media Diversification: Coping With Plenty

New Communication Technologies in Developing Countries

Jarice Hanson
University of Massachusetts
Uma Narula
Indian Institute of Mass Communication

LAWRENCE ERLBAUM ASSOCIATES, PUBLISHERS
1990   Hillsdale, New Jersey   Hove and London

Lawrence Erlbaum Associates, Inc., Publishers
365 Broadway
Hillsdale, New Jersey 07642

Library of Congress Cataloging-in-Publication Data
Hanson, Jarice.
    New communication technologies in developing countries / Jarice
Hanson, Uma Narula.
        p.   cm.—(Communication)
    Includes index.
    ISBN 0-8058-0846-9
    1. Telecommunication—Social aspects—Developing countries.
    2. Information technology—Social aspects—Developing countries.
    I. Narula, Uma, 1933- . II. Title. III. Series: Communication
    (Hillsdale, N.J.)
    TK5102.5.H323 1990
    303.48'33'091724—dc20   90-37766
                                                                 CIP

Printed in the United States of America
10 9 8 7 6 5 4 3 2 1

Contents

Preface

This book is a product of the information revolution. It represents a collaboration of two minds over 26,000 miles—a true product of the information society in itself, and subject to the typical problems of postal services, telephony, and international computer transfer. Despite the problems of hardware and logistics, our goal has been to explore how several countries are responding to the pressures of the information society. We explore the scenarios in these countries by investigating infrastructural development, policies, and social systems, and we propose models of information technologies and society to better reference the differences and similarities among the nations profiled.

We have identified the social technology perspective with the assimilation of technology in lifestyles and social systems. From this perspective we look at the diffusion of technologies with a critical eye for theories of culture lag, diffusion and innovation, technological determinism and liberalism, and within the setting of the cultural context.

This book presumes the reader has some knowledge about the communication technologies, their revolution, development, and cultural contexts. The social technology perspective is a new addition to development studies, and the reader may see how as the global information society comes into focus, the social dimensions are more important than some theories had originally envisioned.

Jarice Hanson
Uma Narula

1

Introduction: Technology in Developing Countries

> *The public policies which mould communications systems are also social policies—by design or default.*
> —Marjorie Ferguson (1986)

The Third World countries are participating in a communication revolution of new, primarily electronic technologies. These technologies may help fight illiteracy, disease, poverty, and other development problems, but they have also created different priorities and issues for these nations. A major issue for developing countries concerns what the communication revolution will do to, and for them. Will they foster communication abundance, strengthen existing technologies, or enhance neocolonial (dependency) forces? What are their technology options for appropriate technopolicies, training, and building an integrated communication infrastructure?

Development studies span a wide range of issues, but the use of media in development has focused much attention on the tools, methods, and impact of messages that create change within a country. For many nations the adoption of telephone, radio, film, and even to some extent, television, was considered to open the possible channels of communication among varied segments of the population. Countries of the Third World have wrestled with the problems of technology transfer, indigenous production of hardware and software, and bilateral or multilateral negotiations with other nations (developed or developing) to make these technologies operational.

The variety of technologies however, has changed for the developing nations. Technologies that were such easy facilitators of entertainment content (i.e., radio, film, and television) are being added to by either large-scale

1

technologies such as the computer or satellite, and the addition of peripheral media such as videocassette recorders or compact discs have supplemented the functions of the traditional media. Today's technology often fosters an even more radical change within traditional societies, and the decision whether to adopt a specific information technology may have immediate implications for the economy, political structure, or social structure of a nation. To be a part of the "Information Revolution" exerts both time, space, and infrastructural pressures beyond those envisioned by traditional media.

Many scholars and researchers have considered how similar or different the information revolution is to the industrial revolution of the past. Goh Sengh Kim (1982) found a corollary to this in the form of an emerging "intellectual technological society" whose components are information and knowledge. The new theories of the value of products and services based on information and knowledge would be different than the conventional economic values, experiences, and judgments, but although technology has been blamed for many of today's ills, it has also been an important factor in humanizing people, and therefore, indispensable for their survival.

The purpose of this book is threefold. The first is to explore the existing media and information technologies in selected developing countries with regard to both hardware and software considerations. Virtually all developing nations have experienced changes due to some forms of media and information technologies, and technological structures have been created through implementation of a wide range of policies. Information technologies add a new dimension to the nation's information capacity, but these tools are often imposed on existing structures. We then explore the advanced technologies' presence and applicability within the confines of the structures already present within the social contexts. Our purpose is not to create structural arguments, but rather to work within the confines of what already exists within the developing nations. Second, we examine the media philosophies and pragmatics included in current media policies to better understand the precedents for information policy. This becomes extremely important for developing nations today because of the political, economic, and cultural dimensions of a greater reliance on technologies that are often produced in industrialized nations, and that must be compatible with technological systems on a global scale. The third purpose of this volume considers how political, economic, cultural, and technological dimensions relate to the diffusion of technology in a society, and examines their cumulative effects on the lifestyles of the individuals. There are often conflicting opinions, attitudes, and beliefs surrounding the ultimate impact of the technology itself, and the amount of change to traditional society that may occur. For this reason we discuss existing structures (both technological and social), and their impact on both the government's perspectives toward the technology, and the considerations by the various segments within the population. The social structures within developing nations are often highly stratified by geography, topography, and transportation. The large rural populations and shifts from rural to urban centers in recent years have strained the resources of many developing nations.

In some countries the notion of power (who has it, who uses it, and who wants it) plays a greater role than in others, but we advocate the position that the availability of technology does not equal social change. It is the patterns of use that concern us, and therefore, we address these problems within cultural contexts, and determine what cultural challenges each nation must face.

MEDIA AND INFORMATION TECHNOLOGIES

The differentiation between media and information technologies is not a significant definitional problem, but it does suggest an important historical dimension. Traditionally, the term *media technology* referred to telephony, radio, and television—all technologies that at one time suggested limited purpose and utility. *Information technology* however, is a loosely defined term and is identified with a wider range of communication technologies such as computers, satellites, and "add-ons" to older media forms by means of video- and audio-cassette recorders, video and audio disc machines, and the broader range of telecommunication technologies that integrate larger, more sophisticated connections such as computer and telephone, telephone and video, and satellite and computer.

Information technology today is basically electronic and is based on integrated circuits or silicon chips. The major two forms of electronic information technology have been termed *telematics,* meaning "big media," and are identified with such technologies as computers, telephone, satellites, television, radio, video, and those that rely on large-scale infrastructures. When we speak of telematic technologies, there is the implicit assumption that we are speaking about both the process of the message transmission as well as the hardware needed to complete the transaction.

The second type of technology has been termed *ethnotronic,* or "small media," such as typewriters, audiocassette recorders, facsimile (FAX) machines, paper copiers, calculators, digital watches, and other more personal types of technologies. All of these information technologies are diverse—crossing boundaries of telematic and ethnotronic technologies. In concert with this diversity is the range of uses supplied by software that integrates computerization, office automation, communication of voice, data, image and text, and artificial intelligence (AI). Although different developing countries represent a range of levels of technological sophistication, it would be appropriate to say that in general, ethnotronic technology in developing countries is stronger and more pervasive than telematic technology. It is the personal nature of ethnotronic technology that de-emphasizes governments' acknowledged importance compared to the development of telematics, but both developed countries and international agencies play significant roles in application, diffusion, and assessment of both ethnotronic and telematic technologies in developing countries.

The new ethnotronic and telematic technologies are establishing a different equilibrium in their societies. The communication revolution has resulted in several levels of communication:

1. communication between humans and machines linked by a technological system,
2. communication between persons through the agency of technological systems,
3. communication between technological systems through the agency of persons, and
4. communication between groups and social systems.

Emerging models today indicate that relationships between and among these levels of communication are both unidimensional and multidimensional. Cinema, radio, television, and video have traditionally taken their places in societies as unidimensional communication media, whereas computers, telephones, FAX networks, and so on, are two-way or multidimensional in the sense that they integrate both wired and nonwired distribution systems, and capitalize on those forms of communication media that have traditionally stressed the agency of the *sender* of communication as predominant over the activity of the *receiver* of the information.

These unidimensional media technologies have created paradoxical situations by giving rise to centralized, pyramidal, hierarchical systems and supersystems, but on the other hand the development of group and network technologies favor decentralization, pluralism, and democracy. These multidimensional technologies have inspired a larger number of scenarios than any other social activity both in developed as well as developing countries because of the complexity of their nature; they are not simply more elaborate clones of earlier communication technologies, but complex systems that have their own cultural characteristics when applied to communication systems.

One of the first infrastructures needed for any societal development was transportation; the second, energy; the third, the ability to communicate over distance, such as that which has developed into a telecommunication infrastructure, including telephone, telex, and data transfer. Because of the importance of the rapid transmission of information, it is necessary now to develop a fourth infrastructure of telematics that combines both the processes and technologies of information transfer (through telecommunications and computers) to facilitate and ensure inexpensive, effective, sufficient, reliable transmission and retrieval of information and knowledge. This raises ergonomic questions of technology–human interaction that address the suitability of the technology for specific tasks. For example, a worker cannot sit at a word processor for hours without a break, and not suffer from eyestrain, backache, or other physiological stress. We must also address the potential problem of dehumanized communication by the use of machines that seemingly take the place of people. These issues are inevitably tied to what each nation determines to be their stake in the information society.

MEDIA TECHNOLOGIES IN DEVELOPING COUNTRIES: PRIORITIES, ISSUES, AND CONCERNS

The new communication technologies are changing the nature of the human environments by offering a wide range of information and communication resources to people. Arthur C. Clarke (1981) saw the potential of new communication technologies unifying a much fragmented world into "one big gossiping family" not withstanding present political and ideological differences. Clarke called these technologies "weapons of peace." Karl Deutsche (1963) viewed the same phenomena as potentially more repressive for their potential to replace traditional police and military operations as keepers of order.

An optimistic (although somewhat naive) projection may be that developing countries may stand to gain the most from new innovations because they are not yet burdened with heavy fixed investments in technology that have become obsolete, or make switching to a new system cost prohibitive. The development of fiber optics as a lower cost alternative to copper cable for telephone distribution is one such example. However, in this context, developing countries have had to address the problem of buying the latest technology or rejecting it in the hopes that a better one will be coming along in the near future. Many of these countries are apprehensive of adopting a form of technology that requires training and knowledge that would lead them into greater technological servitude to a country or corporation. With this consideration, technology is often rejected based on the assumption that the form of technology is unsuitable for the needs of the developing countries. However, it may not be apparent that these countries may need a mix of high, intermediate, and low technologies to meet different needs effectively. Therefore, alternative efforts are needed to transfer and import technologies as well as technical skills and knowledge to indigenously produce technologies according to the country's resources and to participate in developing such technologies in these nations themselves.

There appear to be four major priorities for a developing country to consider with regard to developing a telematic infrastructure (excluding economics, which is discussed later in this chapter):

1. whether to use technological means at all,
2. to formulate appropriate technopolicies,
3. consideration of technology training, and
4. to consider what is necessary for the building of an integrated communication infrastructure.

The first priority of the developing countries is that these new communication technologies (NCTs) should be compatible with the needs, resources, and levels of technical skills of the people. These technologies should be cost effective and practical. Therefore, the important task before developing countries is to assess technological options in terms of public needs, characteristics and actual performance, cost effectiveness, and available country resources. Furthermore, development and utilization of these technologies depends on creating technology awareness, developing applications and levels of skills—perhaps to be called a *social infrastructure*.

The second priority requires that developing countries improve and upgrade any conventional technological systems such as telegraphy, postal services, telephony, or radio. In so doing, the future needs of the nation must be ascertained for growth and development on all scales.

The third priority assumes that outdated technology, technopolicies, and technology training lead to underdevelopment. In such a situation the efficiency is lowered and the percentage of avoidable waste is high. Moreover, outdated technopolicies and substandard technocrats cannot help in developing indigenous growth of high technology.

The fourth priority is building a broad-based, integrated communication infrastructure. At times, the high rates of technologies narrows the number of users (e.g., use of telephone, TV, VCR, and computer). Therefore, the developing countries must opt for cost-effective technologies that enhance what is already available while providing reasonable options for growth.

Along with these priorities, several issues arise such as the suitability of technologies for a developing country that were created for use in a more industrialized world. This poses several questions, as one might assume. Is it possible for developed countries' technologies to fit in with the needs of developing countries? The two worlds differ socioeconomically, culturally, and often ideologically. These problems call for responsive policies for transfer and import of technology, knowledge and training, and consideration of a policy of indigenous production. Ideally, because the developed countries have a greater history with which to determine needs and applicability, they should be better able to construct a mechanism to identify users' needs, skills, and resources. The effectiveness, appropriateness, and value of technology depends on the appropriateness of information being processed, developed, and transferred; its timeliness, quality, relevance, and accountability to actual users' needs and skills. In many cases developed countries are producing technologies in the developing countries themselves for cost effectiveness, adoption of technologies to users' needs, and practicability. This type of manufacturing may provide many benefits, such as jobs, training, and enhancement of the nation's economic base, but concurrent problems such as inequitable wage and price structuring, exploitation, social restructuring, and cultural imperialism also rise to the fore.

As stated earlier, a major concern for developing countries is what communication will hold for them—communication abundance, strengthening of existing communication technologies, or strengthening neo-colonialism (dependency) forces, and decisions are often constrained by historical relationships, economy, education, cultural, and social structures. By a transfer of technology the more industrialized nations may assist the developing countries as well as reinforce consolidation of their (developed countries') economic power and dominance but they may not be willing to transfer their top-level advanced technologies to the developing countries. What they may transfer is only second- or third-level technology, thereby creating even more of a disadvantage for development, and exacerbating colonial legacies of exploitation, cultural domination, or force.

In addition, the need for some advanced-level communication technologies in developing countries may be imperative for development although the availability of technology and access to it may be minimal. The national problems and limitation of resources both material and human thwart the acceptance, absorption, indigenisation, applications, and research in advanced technologies. Even some developing countries that may be just following western technologies blindly may be facing other social, economic, and political implications.

Although there have been many critiques of the willingness, effectiveness, and ability of developing countries to selflessly assist developing nations in these areas, another possible perspective with which to develop as unbiased aid as possible comes from the cooperative efforts of several developed nations through organizations such as UNESCO, the International Telecommunications Union (ITU) or the efforts of the organization established by the Maitland Commission for a partnership among countries of the First, Second, and Third Worlds for a multifaceted, multiideological approach to determining the needs and objectives for developing nations.

The second issue is the need and importance to transfer the technology and the technical skills from developed to developing countries and among developing countries themselves, according to the needs, resources, and technical ambience of the various developing countries. Bharat Karnard (1987) has noted that the developed countries use technology as foreign policy. A specific instance might be that of the United States seeking to capitalize on what it believes is a new trend, particularly in the Third World, of appreciation of scientific and technological advancement as a means to acquire international influence and clout. The Reagan Administration embarked on a conscious use of science and technology as a foreign policy tool, with India, China, and Brazil among the major developing countries and the Association of SouthEast Asian Nations (ASEAN) Group of nations constituting the primary testing grounds for this policy.

In addressing the Congressional Committee Dr. John Montague (1986), scientific adviser to President Reagan said:

> Many developing countries now see scientific and technological capability rather than military might as the one aspect of national character most likely to permit them to leapfrog into the class of nation with significant international political and economic influence and because the U.S.A. is widely perceived as the world leader in this area.
>
> Our nation's scientific and technological expertise and resources have become a powerful policy lever to strengthen our already close partnerships with industrially advanced allies, expanding relations with developing countries and to transform to our advantage the political climate and competition with our adversaries.
>
> The science and technology initiative (STI) with India first agreed in 1982 and reaffirmed in 1985 would act as model enterprises which the U.S. would hope to promote elsewhere in the developing world.

John D. Negroponte (1986), Head of the State Department Office of International Environmental and Scientific Affairs commented that bilateral, multilateral, and other agreements in this field have a particular applicability to support specific types of science and technology activities, maximize political impact, and are important tools in foreign policy.

Because the nature of the present day communication technology is diffusive rather than exclusive, both the developing and developed countries should act together for transfer, import, and development of these technologies. Many Third World countries have begun to participate by assessing their technological needs and resources and have begun to make demands on the developed countries as well as to participate in developing technologies and technical skills.

The Prime Minister of India, Rajiv Gandhi, while addressing the Asia Pacific nations in New Delhi in November 1986 called for a halt to technology dependence and for a reversal of the current trend of overwhelming dependency on industrialized countries for technology. Prime Minister Gandhi indicated that many developing countries today were in fact the leaders in technology in earlier times. To lessen technological dependency on others, the Prime Minister stressed the need for Asia Pacific countries to intensify efforts in the fields of technology transfer, technology adaptations, indigenous technology development, technological orientation among developing countries, and suitable orientation in work ethics.

He also urged developing Economic, Social, Cultural and Political (ESCAP) signatories of the U.N. to see to it that outdated and rejected technologies are not passed on to them and to speed up the process of economic development through the systematic application of technology. In this context he added that the Asian and Pacific Center for Transfer of Technology (APCTT) has a very useful role to play.

The ESCAP executive secretary (1986) recalled that APCTT gained prominence for developing countries in the region since 1984 when the commission's session was devoted to "Technology for Development." This was further reinforced by the 1986 session on "Human Resources Development: Its Technological Dimension." The U.N.'s Committee on technology and development (UNCTAD) – ESCAP's joint interregional symposium organized in New Delhi in April 1987 resulted in many countries' comments that a Southern model of technology transfer that would be more development orientated, compared to the commercial one, should be a priority for implementation. The symposium recognized that some of the developing countries have potential for transfer of technologies but they lack the marketing and infrastructure support.

Apart from the problem of technology access in developing countries there are technology-related structural and behavioral problems as well. The potential for any effectiveness of these technologies depends on political, cultural, economic, software, and technical interventions; and also on how these technologies are institutionalized and utilized.

Beside these interventions, the four other forces that will effect the acceptance of new communication technologies (NCTs) include:

1. the revised concept of communication as more interactive,
2. revolution of more new information institutions,
3. information and social structures to fit in the new communication technologies, and
4. the process of adoption of these technologies.

The NCTs have posited certain priorities, issues, and concerns that call for mutual acceptance, and cooperation of both developed and developing countries. Scant efforts have been made to monitor the impact of new technologies on the Third World when Western technologies are transplanted. Major global environmental concerns, such the atmospheric effects of Chernobyl, Bhopal, and the deteriorating ozone layer have only recently become rallying points for inter- and intranational discussion and activity.

The developed countries have various organizations for technology assessment in their own countries, but what has been lacking is the monitoring of these new technologies and assessing their impact on developing countries. Moreover, most of the developing countries do not have the institutions capable of making their own technology impact analysis.

These deliberations indicate that beside these communication hardware policy options and opportunities, the developing countries are most concerned with the social and psychological side effects of newer communication technologies, the potential social changes resulting from use of new communication technology in concert with the social consequences, and the threat that these technologies pose. For this reason, we refer to the concept of *social technologies.*

SOCIAL TECHNOLOGY

In today's world, we face communication technology challenges and cultural challenges simultaneously. The first relates to the medium and interfacing technologies; the second relates to the ways and means to accept technology in the individual lifestyle and social system—how the communities relate technology to their lifestyles and national identities. In this approach the emphasis is on message content—its quality and meaning as well as the acceptance of communication technology (medium) per se. Thus, these two challenges encompass a revolution in hardware and creativity in software.

The diffusion of communication technologies calls for the development of social technologies. The word "technology" suggests both a way of doing things and the system imposed by that process. Social technology is doing things in such a way that the people's activities contribute to the inevitable changes in the social system. In the context of technological change, the concept of social technology is identified with acceptance of a particular medium as well as the message meaning relayed through the individual and social system. Whenever any new form of technology is introduced, change results. Perhaps the amount of change, and the effect of change may appear to be negligible—but often the impact of change is not felt for a significant period of time—perhaps for generations. From the social technological point of view, the performance demands of technology must fit into existing patterns of human interaction to be meaningful in the particular social system. In order that technological change is accepted by the people of a nation, it must meet the standards of their social traditions that act as guidelines for acceptance as well as censorship of technological changes both by the people and the government. Therefore, the concept of social technology is critical for any form of technological change.

We also need a level of *social competence* to deal with communication and technological change. Social competence is identified with modes of combat, drawing on cultural resources (cultural resources are stories, institutions, and traditions of a society) to fit technological changes and willingness to put these cultural resources at risk. The social competence and cultural dimensions of technology are closely related and we can expect a threefold impact: (a) the impact of "technology" of communication per se on cultural values, (b) the impact of cultural values on communication media content, and (c) the impact of media content on cultural values.

Critical theory takes society as a starting point for the measurement of change rather than a particular medium as the starting point from which to evaluate change. Therefore, in the context of the diffusion of communication technology and its resulting change, the focus should be on *social technologies* as they identify the needs, potential of new media technologies, and the media influences within society. The new media technology may be, in a sense, overcommitted to societal development. Althusser's (1971) attention to the ideological functions performed by media through ideological state apparatuses (ISA) addresses how ISAs legitimize power structures by shared meanings and the cultivation of ideology.

The technology theory of society treats media as generation specific. Society has to decide at which point which media should serve the society's needs and values. The needs and classified use of media could be an ideologically message-oriented, data-oriented, and information-oriented media. Therefore, the social technologies are society specific and include the perspective and priorities of the government elites and the masses—the concerns and problems of the society as a whole. The acceptance and effectiveness of these technologies depend on such social technology interventions as political, economic, cultural, and technical capacities of countries and their attitude toward technology.

The essential components of the social technology concept include process, forms, adoption, implications, and strategies. The social impact of technologies may be viewed from several perspectives such as individual, family and community, and national and international (see Fig. 1.1). Although these interact, each poses different sets of problems.

Social technology can be viewed as the social innovation aspect of technology. The process of social technology is assimilating the social aspect of technology in the lifestyle of individuals and in the social system. There are forms of social technology through which social aspects of technology functions are expressed (e.g., industries, universities, and government re-

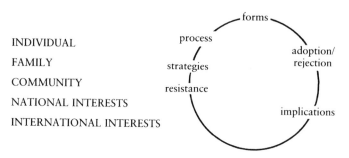

FIG. 1.1.   The social technology model.

cords). The adoption of technology is a social decision, therefore it has social implications.

The current social technology strategy in many developing countries is to let rural communities adopt technology and diffuse technology at a grassroot level. Within this example, the social technology perspective takes into consideration:

1. how the new communication technologies effect the individual life-style in terms of quality of life, family relationships and activities, social relationships, gender-role stratification, knowledge growth, leisure-time utilization, values of life, and information-seeking behavior;

2. how the new communication technologies effect the social system by increasing or decreasing the gap between information rich and information poor; changes in community-based activities, and interest of specific segments of the society;

3. how the new communication technologies will lead to more involvement, access, participation at various communication levels both by users and management through communication content, style, control, management access by the users and vice versa; and participation in production.

Newer forms of communication technology like satellites, computers, and interactive video, help in expansion, revitalization, and new uses of the traditional forms of technology. Both old and new forms of technology undoubtedly co-exist at least in some forms. Changes in communication technology produce changes in modes of thought, social organization, and patterns of leisure activities. For example, earlier radio, film, and television has often been treated as primarily entertainment media in developing countries. Now they may be utilized predominantly as educational and prosocial agents. There are changes in media-related social organizations also, such as radio forums, tele-clubs, womens' discussion groups, and video parlors, to mention only a few.

At present, interactive media has changed the concept of source and receiver. It has become rather *participant* oriented. Such technological changes will create new research needs and theoretical models, social psychological side effects, actual social consequences, and potentialities for social change.

In developing countries, the social technologies are being created by government planners so that technologies are assimilated in people's lifestyles and their social systems. This follows a diffusion model to diffuse technology among people and to create scientific ambience to assimilate technology in their lifestyle.

The diffusion of technology is created by: (a) creating awareness of technologies that are relevant and useful, (b) demonstrating that old technologies are outdated, (c) reorienting people to change their attitudes toward old and new technologies, and (d) making decisions after diagnosing and evaluating their needs (more of the diffusion process is discussed in chapter 3). When scientific ambience is created it helps to encourage technological needs of the individual, community, and society. Both media and social technologies legitimize each other.

Communication Technology: Cultural Challenge

The creation of social technologies poses a cultural challenge for preserving the cultural identity and values of the particular society. Technology is a component of culture and is understood in its cultural context. Technology choice is within a system—never within a vacuum. The communicators in developing countries identify media technology development and expansion with prosocial roles, and they are perpetually concerned whether media technologies will be preservers or destroyers of cultural values. Will these technologies encourage a breakdown of traditional values and support mediocre and substandard values? Or, while preserving cultural identity, will they erode cultural vitality, internal diversity, and intercultural understanding? Erosion of cultural vitality may be identified with a process of stereotyping, a breakdown of cultural forms, and reduction in opportunities for minority cultures.

There has to be a positive relationship between technology and cultural development enriching the cultural resources and respect for cultural diversity. This is necessary, particularly in developing societies that are basically pluralistic. Thus, media technologies become culture specific. They are not universally applicable and must be adapted to the needs of different cultures, and they must be acquired and introduced with a concern for levels and regions with different variations. Some authors assume that people live in "split-level" cultures created by media technologies. What matters is not abstract potentiality of media technologies but the value that is attributed to them locally. Technology is not "constant" but a political, economic, and cultural acquisition, with short-term and long-term effects and consequences.

Cultural Context

Culture determines in part, the types of communication we engage in and the appropriateness of models. Many of these models evolve into social institutions that have powerful social effects and act within the cultural context to reinforce existing values, norms, or practices while at the same time introducing the potential for change. Many of the problems of communication are linked to problems of communities in which we live. It is not enough to attempt to censor or prohibit communication, but it is necessary to create the type of environment compatible with the dominant ideology of technology of mass media if it is to be used effectively.

Communication is, however, always in a cultural context because whether it is interpersonal or mediated communication, it is presented, received, reacted, and acted upon. To paraphrase technical jargon, a "signal of compliance" must be given to indicate that a message has been received. (The choice not to act upon the message is equal to an action in the same way that not to decide something already presumes a decision has been made.) There will always be three major actors involved in a communication/cultural context in Third World countries; the government, media community, and the people.

The effectiveness of a particular technology depends on the dominant cultural ideology. For example, in a country like India, the cultural ideology toward technology is decidedly prosocial, and the application favors the medium of television as a purveyor of the ideology. As a result, more efforts are made to develop TV technology rather than other technologies that do not enhance cultural goals. In the United States, the cultural ideology of labor-saving devices (such as the computer) indicates that there may be more flexibility and incentive to produce more computer technologies than enable television to experience growth and development. U.S. government politics toward deregulation are an indispensable proof of which technologies the government sees as having growth potential, and which ones the government deems not as important.

Economic Factors

The most obvious problem with regard to using technology for any purpose, is the cost. Large infrastructures require financial commitment for maintenance, yet many of the Third World nations lack the ability to invest in the size and quality of components necessary for global communication. This constraint places a heavy burden on development—one that has a significant impact on any and all policies initiated by a government. In some countries, most noticeably in Latin America, the economic constraints have led to some rather unusual financing arrangements among private and public, national and international interests.

More and more, technological development is being used as a reason for, and an excuse for heavy economic investments in defense spending. Most governments give the greatest amount of leeway in terms of research and development to military branches. These investments are often touted as necessary for the defense of a country, but complications and implications go far beyond a strategic investment.

A related issue is that the problems with technology often seem to require technological solutions. Are nations that invest money into technologies that can be used for defense asking for an opportunity to prove those technologies work? Do governments that invest in defense technologies do so at the expense of more basic problems such as poverty, disease, and hunger?

The notion of communication as a basic human right has become popular since the Universal Declaration of Human Rights was advocated in 1948. Technologies in many cases, particularly in the area of telephony, are no longer considered luxury appliances, but rather necessities. These technologies, and the means to make them work, must be cost accessible to the general public.

Similarly, although nations may have stated policies toward the use of technologies, the practices must rely on commensurate elements of production, distribution, and reception. For example, the Indian government's plan to use television for prosocial messages would not work if the population did not have television receivers available and the methods of transmission were not reliable.

Two important issues then become juxtaposed: technology and economics, and economics and social needs. This book investigates the relationships among these issues within a case study context for nations that have similar concerns. But for individual reasons, these nations have taken different viewpoints and actions toward meeting the challenges of communication in an information age at the national level, but also at the level that affects the individual in society.

SUMMARY

The problem of development thus incorporates technological, economic, and social dimensions. It is impossible to address many questions that cut across the specificity required by each developing nation; therefore, a cultural context is necessary to better understand the policies, practices, and impact of changes as they are experienced by various nations.

The requirements for support of telematic and enthnotronic technologies
are not the same, but they are related. Although many developing nations
have placed emphasis on the large-scale infrastructural needs of telematic
technologies, the ethnotronic technologies have often introduced change
at a greater rate of speed, due to their personal nature, and the lack of
infrastructural organization needed to make them work.

However, the social technologies used to diffuse any technology and
their impact on a culture address the process of development at a more
fundamentally pragmatic level; the social systems and their relationship to
the information technologies is thus, the point of entry for our discussions
of developing nations and their role in an information society.

The Power of Information Technology

How do we know there are computers in those boxes? Maybe they're full of rocks.—statement of an Indian official having observed a shipment of new computers. No skilled individuals had been hired to install them.

There are many notions of what the information society is, or could be. Scenarios of the future predict a range of possibilities, but separating fact from fiction is a difficult task because there are strong precedents that give credence to even the most outlandish predictions. In this chapter we investigate some of the potential for change, the large, international agencies that are powerful actors in the use of information technology (IT) for global development, and the elements of change that may override specific scenarios.

PROPHETS OF CHANGE

There are many images of the power of information projected by those who talk of information societies and information revolutions. One theme predicts wondrous images of technologically instant access to appropriately managed information enabling more effective human action. The other theme is calamitous—images of population subgroups without access, getting poorer while the rich get richer. In reality, however, the extreme polarities of utopia or dystopia are far more likely to encompass varieties of change in each society, felt by different individuals at different times. The following authors have all contributed significant approaches to understanding the possibilities.

Majid Tehranian (1988, pp. 36–37) described four scenarios that are much more rooted in historic notions and ideologies. The four call into question scenarios as those of continuity, reform, collapse, and/or transformation, all of which describe attitudes toward the greater use of information technology by present and emerging political groups. His thesis is particularly interesting in light of recent trends that have seen the following:

1. ideas of past trends, that is, the postindustrial or information society continuing to expand its domain from world centers to the peripheries (continuity scenario);

2. a call for a new world economic, communication, and information order, and continual negotiations between North and South (reform scenario);

3. the failure of peripheral nations, that is, Iran, the Philippines and Latin America to argue that the system will first break down at its weakest links, and that uneven processes of economic growth in some industries can have disastrous social and political consequences (collapse scenario); and

4. the contributions of 200 years of utopian thinking in response to the onslaught of world modernisation and industrialization, that is, the principles of the Green movements around the world, Liberation theology, Grassroots movements, etc. (transformation scenario).

John Lent (1986) wrote that myths are built around what information technology could actually do, and therefore, he reminded us that many of these scenarios are possibilities, rather than definitive predictions. He said that some of the myths prophesy that new information technology will lead to the development of a global village, others portend of new information technologies that will serve international understanding, peace, and brotherhood. Some myths portray information technology that will lead to increased independence and promotion of democratic ideals, yet others promote technology as the salvation of the Third World masses, and therefore, more information made available through bigger communication systems is a goal to be sought. This last myth considers technology neutral—which is a notion highly suspect by many authors, and one that we discuss later in this chapter.

Other myths cited by Lent pay homage to history by indicating that because new information technology has worked in the industrialized world, therefore it will work in the Third World. The power of myths and popular predictions cannot be overlooked as we investigate how, why, and if information technology will affect a given culture or create a new one.

One of the themes surrounding future predictions deals with what constitutes "information." Perhaps one of the most well-known interpretations of
the information society comes from Daniel Bell (1973) who defined it as a
society that trades information as a commodity, by changing the economic
sector from producing goods to producing information and services. In
Bell's vision of the information society, occupational distribution would be
dominated by a professional and technical class and the axial principle—the
centrality of theoretical knowledge would be the source of information and
policymaking. The decision-making process would depend on the creation
of a new "intellectual technology" and the future would be controlled by
technology and technology assessment.

Brenda Dervin (1986) indicated that some core assumptions about the
nature of information have guided our thinking on the subject. When and if
information is regarded as a resource, it is assumed that this information is
objective, and can be measured against the reality that it is supposed to
represent. Similarly, access can also be measured. Such assumptions have
lead to information systems becoming less and less useful. These assumptions
do not require the system to be responsive to human needs, and these
assumptions have had some impact on the use of new technologies for
communication purposes both in the area of policymakers who see little or
no feedback from the integration of media technologies, and in the realm of
social critics who see media as linear and deterministic. This has resulted in
several permutations of ideas that limit the potential of any technological
use.

Information technology may produce a new kind of society or it may
foster a continuation of previous industrial development. Herbert Schiller
(1983) and Raymond Williams (1983) argued that an industrial society is
not different from an information society but this change is another form of
industrialization and capitalism.

Scenarios such as these raise several issues for nations finding their way
(by default or choice) into the information society. One important issue
raised by the predictions of authors like Bell, Williams, and Schiller, concerns
the nature of work and the payment for goods and services. If indeed
information becomes a commodity, how is it traded? Some predictions call
attention to the "piece work" principle of the assembly line that could very
well be adapted to the number and amount of information processed by a
clerk (Martin, 1981). Payment could ostensibly reflect the number of forms
completed, amount of data transferred, or jobs completed. Although scaling
this idea to developing nations may not appear to have tremendous initial
consequences, other notions of the information society do.

A "Third World" perspective could be that such as the one provided by
Umesao (1963), who stated that in developing societies the agriculture,
fisheries, cattle breeding, and so forth, are *endoderm industries,* which are

basic and maintain life for the individual. *Mesoderm industries* move and produce, such as transportation, construction, and manufacturing. Finally, there are *ectoderm industries*, like those of information, communication, culture, and education. This perspective is particularly interesting because it places the developing nations in a framework that focuses on traditional practices more than on the continuity of industrialization.

One other intriguing possibility for the future can be seen by the work of Jacques Ellul (1985), who discredited many of the popular myths, conceptions, and scenarios and view the use of information technologies from a perspective that is not grounded in either the superutopian or dystopian (see Table 2.1).

Ellul of course, is not suggesting that technology is value free, but rather, that many prophets of IT choose to enter the debate from a philosophical perspective that negates what we know about the history of technology use.

CHARACTERISTICS OF INFORMATION TECHNOLOGY

Information technology is one of the most dynamic and controversial areas of science and technology due to its rapid pace of change, the emphasis placed for economic growth and for national security, and the pervasive or "core" nature of the technology and its effects. The social goals of science policy have been to improve the quality of life, knowledge for knowledge's

TABLE 2.1
Preconceived Ideas About Mediated Information

1. Information is power: false, because much is wrong, or it goes too fast to be digested.
2. The flow of information replaces the flow of goods: illogical.
3. An excess of information in forms: not true because of information overload.
4. Modern information systems endlessly spread bad news while reducing the depth of the news transparency: modern people live in a world of fiction that ignores the positive aspects of news.
5. Everything is possible with a computer: wrong, it can only handle binary logic; spirituality, morality, qualitative, and human relationships cannot be converted to binary logic.
6. The world is a global village: this can only happen when all information is relevant to the individuals, which is not the case today.
7. Dialogue is possible: mass communication surpresses dialogue.
8. Dialogue is impossible: communication technologies are merely gadgets.
9. The mass media foster democracy: the division between information rich and information poor divides societies.

Note: Abstracted from Ellul (1985).

sake, equity, and education. The social goals in technology policy have been mainly economic well-being, national security, and technological leadership. The information society does not re-create the wheel. Rather, it draws on the techniques and applications of technology that, in turn, suggest new values and principles that exist along with the old ones. These techniques and applications have to do with the unique characteristics of technology, and indicate what "machine-like" control could add or change, with regard to traditional practices.

Hanson (1987) has suggested that there will undoubtedly be three new principles emerging from conditions of a greater use of electronic technologies. First, the issue of *control* will be significantly greater in the future; control by the user of the technological system and by the acknowledgement of the types of control exerted by the technical system itself. The idea of control ranges from who has access to the system and can use it (for whatever purposes) to the type of information that is stored, transferred, or transmitted by the technology. One of the greatest concern for people of all nations regarding control and technological systems has to do with privacy. This may include information that is stored about a person or the person's actions as well as government documents and national security measures, and brings in questions of human and national rights.

Panoptic Power

An ultimate example of the dynamics of control with IT has been outlined by Michel Foucault (1979) who recalled the architectural innovation tauted by Jeremy Bentham called the Panopticon. The 1787 plan for the structure included a 12-sided polygon that would provide "universal transparency" for the control and viewing of individuals who had "flouted, thwarted, or otherwise escaped social authority" (Zuboff, 1988, p. 320). This structure would be used for convicts, paupers, students, asylum inmates, workers, and other deviants; and provided a work environment in which the presence of outside observation was always a possibility, but could not be easily detected by the workers at their jobs.

> Bentham laid down the principle that power should be visible and unverifiable. Visible: the inmate will constantly have before his eyes the tall outline of the central tower from which he is spied upon. Unverifiable: the inmate must never know whether he is being looked at at any one moment; but he must be sure that he may always be so. . . . In the peripheric ring, one is totally seen, without ever seeing; in the central tower, one sees everything without ever being seen. (Foucault, 1979, pp. 201 – 203)

A closer approximation between IT and Panopticon may be inferred from Zuboff (1988):

The Panopticon represents a form of power that displays itself automatically
and continuously. . . . Panopticon produces the twin possibilities of observation
and control. . . . The allure of the panoptic world view is, above all, the promise
of certain knowledge based upon the totality of observation it affords. (p. 321)

Panoptic power is similar to the control over information functions by
any one of the information technologies—but particularly over interactive
technologies such as computers and peripheral equipment (i.e., Level III
and above videodiscs). Hierarchical organizational structures that approach
these levels of interactivity with a knowledge and appropriate techniques to
measure and acknowledge control are needed—but rare. Indeed, to expect
governments, policymakers, and users of IT to be able to extract themselves
from traditional practices embedded in ways of doing things in their societies,
is a big expectation. However, some developing nations are surprisingly
better adapted to accommodate these knowledge constructs, even if they
have little access to the technologies themselves.

The second principle for the information age as articulated by Hanson
(1987) is the notion of *entropy*. Any technological system has a measure of
"noise" or drop-out that impedes the efficient handling of the system. On a
macroscale, entropy can be evaluated as that which is lost in a file, or
message. On a microscale, entropy can impede the message and distort its
meaning.

The concept of *information overload* relates directly to the amount of
entropy in a transaction with IT. Information overload subverts the typical
assumption that more information is better than no information, or little
information by overpowering us with more information than we can use, or
store. As a result, the overload is lost. van Cuilenburg (1987) warned that
an information society may not be an informed society specifically because
having access to a lot of data does not necessarily mean people are well
informed. The law of diminishing returns suggests that in an environment
where little information is available, it is more highly valued; but the more
information available, the less beneficial and more expensive it becomes (as
well as less useful). Curras (1987) elaborated on this notion in his description
of the human information system as a sieve that floods if too much information is put into it. The information-processing unit becomes saturated to the
point where the person's interest in the information diminishes.

The final principle discussed by Hanson is the idea of *precision* required
by advanced technological systems. The exact measurements, read-outs,
linear programs, and quantification of time is alien to most developing
nations and contradicts notions of a "collective consciousness" present in
many oral societies. Precision is a principle dictated by technological systems—without it, the system may technically not work, or, it can create
frustration for users without great technological literacy. Precision is also a

necessary component of the technical system itself, taking the processes of electrical engineering to their most efficient means. Still, this type of technologically determined precision may be devalued or overlooked by some societies.

AGENTS OF CHANGE

In the adoption process of new technologies, each nation experiences three phases of the information revolution: (a) the technological development phase, (b) the phase of software that makes use of the developed technologies, and (c) the diffusion of information in the society.

Can a developing country determine the type of information technology for itself and the type of product service it wants? Yes, provided there is an alternative choice available and known. International cooperation is necessary for promoting communication networks in developing countries, but rather than withholding technologies, developed countries should, and in some ways do support developing countries in assimilating technology. There are several international and intranational agencies that have identified the problems of the inequity of technologies, and lack of planning expertise. Although each of these agencies can be viewed as political entities as well as humanitarian concerns, they have all taken steps to help Third World nations compete (at least on a limited scale) with other nations of the world. The following organizations are only a few of the largest agents of inter- and intranational assistance and organization.

The ITU

The International Telecommunications Union (ITU) was formed in 1865 when 20 European nations met in Paris to sign an agreement called the International Telegraph Convention with the express purpose of regulating telegraph communication over international borders. Within 10 years its purview extended to regulate telephone traffic, and by the time radio began to pose a frequency problem, many other governments also become involved. As of 1932, "the wired and wireless unions merged under a single International Telecommunications Convention and the ITU was created" (Codding, 1979, p. 357).

The ITU concerns itself with planning, administration, technical standards, and global frequency allocations of the electromagnetic spectrum. Several regional meetings are held on varying 3- to 8-year schedules, and world meetings such as the World Administrative Radio Conference (WARC) are held every 20 years.

The 12th Plenipotentiary Conference of the ITU was held in Nairobi in

1983, at which time plans were made to take the ITU into the 1990s. These plans included a number of goals to help the ITU be more responsive to the needs of third world nations, such as:

- a change in the ITU financial structure so that rich nations can contribute more money, and the Third World nations less, than before;
- an increase in ITU's Administrative Council from 36 to 41 members;
- adoption of Arabic as one of the official languages (joining English, Chinese, Spanish, French, and Russian);
- a review of the long-term future of the International Frequency Registration Board (IFRB) and ITU policies for planning and allocating frequencies; and
- recommendations for strengthening technical cooperation and assistance to developing nations through a better regional ITU presence in the Third World (Howell, 1984).

UNESCO

The United Nations Educational, Scientific and Cultural Organization (UNESCO) was established in 1946. Although the organization has provided assistance in several forms to developing nations, the general goals have traditionally been approached through the designation of "development decades." Therefore, the four-decade missions of UNESCO have included:

- 1950–1960: service as a low budget catalyst for the reconstruction of communication facilities and networks ravaged by World War II;
- 1960–1970: the development of communication facilities and training of personnel in the emerging nations through the aid of UN sources;
- 1970–1980: promotion of the new technologies of communication— especially satellites; and
- 1980–1990: emphasis is shifting from material assistance toward helping nations and regions develop communication policies and standards, identify long-range objectives, and formulate decision-making mechanisms.

UNESCO and the UN have been active participants in funding and facilitating dialogue in and among developing nations to help these countries formulate plans and procedures for better, more culturally responsive reactions and planning for domestic and international information systems. The case study chapters in this book further elucidate on some of the specific programs both of these organizations have facilitated.

INTELSAT and INTERSPUTNIK

The International Telecommunications Satellite Organization (INTELSAT) was formed in 1964 to regulate and foster international satellite use in the free and nonaligned countries of the world. With emphasis on making satellite transponder space available to countries that cannot pay for its services, INTELSAT has arranged for a time-sharing procedure through 11 satellites, 224 earth stations, and 125 locations for partial service in 105 countries. The services include voice, telegraph, telex, data, and television transmissions.

Similarly, INTERSPUTNIK is the Soviet satellite system for international use and transponder sharing in and among Soviet nations and others.

The Maitland Commission

Although the organizations just discussed all provide some services to the less-developed nations of the world, critics have found all of them to be lacking in some ways. The Independent Commission for World-Wide Tele-communications Development chaired by Sir Donald Maitland, which reported results of a continuous "supranational" dialogue among nations of the North and South, found that "up to now the flow of assistance from richer to poorer [nations] has not increased and in some cases has declined in real terms" (Maitland, 1985, p. 97).

The Commission found that indeed, the developing countries have even greater problems today than the aforementioned agencies had originally envisioned, or had determined as priority areas in development. The real aim of the developing nations is increasing self-reliance, but as many of these experience greater national and external debt, geographic problems, and a response to "interested" industrialized-world technology suppliers who often treat the developing world as a dumping ground for obsolete or incompatible technologies—problems have become exacerbated.

The Independent Commission outlined 30 recommendations toward redressing the problems of expanding telecommunications in the developing world, all of which would require participation and cooperation of industrialized nations. Although the implementation of these recommendations will take time, the importance of the Commission's work in preparing an arena for dialogue external to those organizations that have already dealt with these issues under the aegis of more overtly political groups, is notable and vital to addressing the wide range of development problems in the area of IT.

INTERPLAY OF MEDIA AND SOCIAL DEVELOPMENT:
IT POLICY IMPLICATIONS

While discussing the implications of technology policies in Third World countries, Hamelink (1983) argued that the strong oligopoly in the production of information technology makes importing countries also usually lack the expertise for the assessment and integration of information technology. At the same time, there is a drive among Third World nations to create some form of information capacity. This is happening usually in a totally uncontrolled manner guided by ad hoc decisions. Although some nations do indeed receive counsel, assistance, or some other means of support by the agents just mentioned, it is also imperative for Third World countries to have policies that give protection against foreign economic impositions with its implied political and cultural agenda. At the same time, there should be an effort to build an infrastructure harnessing available resources to enable future self-reliance.

There seems to be a general anxiety about missing the "information revolution" among Third World countries. And as a consequence, the majority of the policy decisions relate to the spending of public funds on the acquisition of the latest generation technology whether the country is ready for that advanced technology or not to reap its benefits.

Halloran (1986) has constructed a persuasive argument for more socially relevant research that proposes that considerations of the effects of IT (and policies for it) must be treated as more holistic and viewed with an eye for international implications. His argument for more socially relevant research is indicative of lessons learned from prior activities in development. Although we may still speak of "new" technologies, the "newness" is relative. We have learned through a variety of contexts in many countries that (what we will call) "old" technologies, such as telephony, radio, and television have taught decision makers valuable lessons in the areas of cultural and information sovereignty, imperialism, and cultural transfer. Many types of communication gaps and information imbalances have been experienced but none greater than those felt by means of satellite communication and in some cases, the growing distribution of videocassettes (legal and illegal).

The impact of these cultural communications media cannot be overlooked, but fear of technology and software can also hinder effective use of these technologies or others for specific uses that may be beneficial to a nation. The overall objective for cultivating an IT culture is to educate the general public and the governments involved to be familiar with a new environment that includes new technologies.

National Systems and Policies

Information is necessary for development of national and international identity. The flow of information is through communication technologies from individual to individual, from groups to groups, government to government; government to people, and vice versa. There are technological and human sociocultural variables involved in the flow of information that disseminates information to educate people whether it be for consumerism, political, or cultural propaganda. Within these parameters, nations have attempted to form different policies, and have measured accountability on different criteria. The most common forms of feedback to the government to monitor the effectiveness of any use of technology are through technological assessment and innovation policy—which has a "feedback loop" to measure impact.

Certainly one of the most conceptually useful models for understanding the relationship among technology, individuals, and society is provided by the *diffusion of innovations* (Rogers, 1986), which discusses both the innovation and implementation phases of adopting new technologies in an organization. The model includes elements of prior conditions, knowledge of communication channels, persuasion, decision-making, implementation, and confirmation of the innovation-decision process. Elements such as the means of economic support, knowledge of an existing infrastructure in a communication application context, and social acceptance and/or criticism are also integral to understanding the complete process of instituting change within a nation.

These are the areas all too often neglected in the practice of governmental implementation and diffusion plans, and policies created to foster such activity. For this reason, many new diffusion plans in developing countries are treated as though they are pilot projects; when the desired results are not seen immediately, the continued development of the plans may be scrapped for lack of immediate return.

The two most common concepts of planning policies for the diffusion of innovations (particularly in the area of IT) have been technology assessment and innovation policy. Ropohl (1983) has differentiated the two:

> Innovation policy is, so to say, an accelerating force, whereas technology assessment may be regarded as a decelerating factor with respect to technical development. . . . Innovation policy is exclusively oriented to economic factors. (p. 83)

> Technology assessment may be defined as a field of research which, in an anticipatory way, analyzes technical innovations, calculates their consequences for the environment and for society, checks the expected results with regard to relevant values, and makes recommendations based on these studies to

the responsible decision makers in business and politics. Thus, technology assessment is designed not to prevent all innovations, but to select out of the abundance of feasible innovations, the actually desirable ones and to slow down technical development wherever it could become dangerous. (p. 84)

Much of the controversy in determining appropriate technopolicies in developing countries has recognized the importance of constructing strong social policies for acceptance and use of IT. This is a lesson that the Third World can teach the industrialized world—but would anyone listen?

Diffusion of Social Thought Toward IT

The phrase "you can't teach an old dog new tricks," has some relevance for IT use as well. As a result, perhaps the most important agency to inculcate information and technological awareness is the school. The promotion of IT culture at the school level is believed to have far-reaching implications for society. Not only are the present day students to become the active IT generation in the future, they are also expected to be able to play a key role in bringing IT culture to the home and the community. Needless to say, teachers must first be able to conceptualize the wide range of possibilities and themselves cannot fear or evade ITs. This requires a program of teacher education, and additional adult education programs to facilitate new jobs brought about by IT.

Although schools are one place where a "progressive" movement toward IT may be fostered, other social organizations can facilitate positive attitudes toward IT too. In many countries, the tourism boards (government owned, or privatized) have often ushered in computerized travel and accommodation arrangements.

These two examples, however, also indicate one other problem. Only those people who can *afford* to let their children go to school, take courses themselves, travel or participate in the tourism industry, or, take advantage of hospitals, banks, and so on, are in the environments where IT can be viewed in a positive light. The reality is that most of the people of the Third World are in rural areas, often untouched by educational opportunities, electrification, or other means that would bring them in touch with IT. The information technologies then, are often the tools of the wealthy, the elites, or of the government bureaucrats; all of whom generally live in urban areas. Social thought then, can be cultivated at these levels, but their very presence risks marginalizing certain segments of the population even more than their present circumstances. Almost exclusively, IT *begins* within a nation as an urban tool. There are however, some notable exceptions, which we discuss further in following chapters.

Lessons From Developed Countries: To Regulate or Not?

Traditionally, policies in industrialized nations have taken two avenues toward regulation of communication industries: some have taken the free-market economics route (e.g., the United States), which has set up a system of limited regulation based on competitive market principles. A more common tradition has been that of other industrialized nations (e.g., European nations), which have regulated communication industries through direct government ties provided by PTTs (Offices of Post, Telephone and Telecommunications). This latter practice has also been used by most colonies of European nations and other countries that have determined stricter regulation as necessary.

However, a relatively recent trend in deregulation, privatization, and nonregulation of communication technologies in industrialized nations has begun to have an impact upon countries of the third world as well. These practices are due in large part to the increasing internationalization of information technologies and the movement of information across national boundaries.

The practice of *deregulation*—a movement away from government intervention in the determination and function of industries, had become a worldwide phenomenon throughout the 1980s in liberal–conservative governments who wanted to reduce the cost of government by reducing government regulation expenditures (Hills, 1986). The Reagan, Thatcher, Mulroney, and Nakasone governments all experienced massive deregulation of industries—but what has replaced deregulation in all countries other than the United States is the *privatization* of formerly regulated industries.

Privatization becomes an attractive option when the operations of regulation become too large for the government to handle. In many countries experiencing privatization, the costs incurred by the government require cuts elsewhere in the budget—usually to social programs. Industrialized nations have economic infrastructures that may be able to accommodate some of these reallocations, particularly when the private businesses and governments have complementary goals, but Third World nations seldom have stable cooperative structures, and therefore privatization occurs for other reasons.

Privatization is growing, particularly in the nations of South America, Africa, and Asia, where state-owned assets are being sold to the private sector either because the government cannot afford the operations of the industries, or because the market may be too small for more than one enterprise to operate profitably. For these nations, it may be necessary to grant monopoly status to the private concern, or to make concessions on import restrictions. Either way, the capacity for the developing nation to develop indigenous technologies or produce for export purposes becomes a problem. Similarly, the private operation may not complement indigenous cultural goals—by the nature of the owner, or goals that may be incompatible with the desires of both the government and masses. Undoubtedly, however, the societies that do see ITs as more than just economic variables or political levers, have a position of understanding the wider range of possibilities for social change by and with IT. The model suggested then, posits IT as the central concern for a discussion of the nature of knowledge, techniques for application, and a measure of control in a society (see Fig. 2.1).

Ethnotronic Technologies

The "small media" of ethnotronic technologies are often entries on a more social level to a broad membership in an information society. Personal-use technologies are often nonthreatening introductions to those concepts of power and control so easily identifiable on a larger scale.

Therefore, the dynamics of low-cost, portable, and personal technologies cannot be overlooked as a major factor in increasing the "mediated" world of the individual in any society. Yet, governments have been lax to suggest any policies other than deterrent policies (usually based on trade and legal grounds) for the diffusion of these products.

We suggest that policies toward ethnotronic technologies not be considered "stepchild" problems, but that the nature of these ITs should be regarded as important for educating and providing a "technological sense of place" for members of society who may have little access to the government decision makers. In an era of increasingly difficult development due to inequalities in national wealth and in global information distribution, small media may indeed suggest important links for policies and practices that make sense, and have social support.

SUMMARY

The information society is then, a society that posits all new concepts in a world burdened by traditional thinking and means of action. But the information technologies available today (both big and small) challenge traditional notions and practices. Who finds a way to work within the

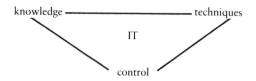

FIG. 2.1.   Placement of information technology in society's transformation.

information society? The answers are complex, but the investigation is illuminating.

One important concept, however, is that information technology relies on a global grid for international use. Therefore, certain agencies that require cooperation must be consulted. We then can see how any one nation's desire, decision, or trial with ITs, inevitably links that nation to a larger, global system. The changes within one nation could ostensibly have ramifications for the rest of the world. Thus, there is no such thing as a "small" change in a society learning to live with IT; but the amount of change in the society may take many years to become known, and understood.

Theories and Applications of Information Technologies

*However confident any society may be of having grasped the histori-
cal and contemporary essential of communication problems, it may
well discover in the next decade, or at furthest in the next century,
that other technological advances have produced unforseen effects,
uncertainties, and imponderables.*

—Sean MacBride (1980)

Many of the theories that have guided development theorists concerned
unidirectional media; that is, large infrastructurally supported systems (such
as radio or television) that could easily become tools of entertainment,
due to their one-way processing of messages. Even telephony was viewed
primarily as an emergency tool, rather than as a medium that would facilitate
social interaction. Today's information technology challenges some of the
earlier assumptions of the role of technology within a developing nation.

INFORMATION TECHNOLOGY AND CHANGE

In this chapter we discuss some of the conceptualizations, theories, and
models that have contributed to the positions taken by several of the prophets
discussed in chapter 2. At different times throughout history certain ways
of thinking about the world dominated intellectual thought and attitudes
toward cultural change.

In conceptualizing the role of media in a developing nation we must
understand the role of tradition, in which the role of social groups may be

even more important practically, than concepts of even political constraints or economy. All media technologies have the capacity to change traditional notions of time and space—concepts that have guided the individual's relationship to his or her environment throughout history in any cultural context. Therefore, it is necessary to realize that *change* is the most significant factor in instituting new practices by means of media technologies.

Change also is a difficult variable to describe because it affects different individuals within their social groups in an individual way; the subjectivity of change and the experience might be articulated in common terms, but felt or perceived at a greater level. There may also be a "sleeper" effect as it were, with the impact of change felt at different times by the same individuals. As a result, change could be viewed as the centrifugal force of media adaptation, with traditional practices the centripetal force, each contributing to the knowledge, social practices, and the individual's reaction to society.

In Fig. 3.1, *change* is positioned between tradition and other internal factors that influence development. The change "wheel" is not an even one; it changes shape according to the centrifugal and cetripetal forces exerted by other dynamics as the wheel turns. At some times the wheel spins more rapidly than at other times. At times, more change is felt by some factors than others. One certainty is that all factors (traditional and current) will experience some aspect, or effect of change.

We can easily see the political dimension of instituting change through media technologies. For example, Iran's contractual agreement with the U.S. firm of AT&T to develop a more advanced telephone system was abandoned in 1983 when the United States placed trade sanctions against Iran. Because of the telephone system already in place, Iran could not turn to another supplier of a telephone system, and therefore, the Iranian telephone system has been unable to grow or expand. Even if Iran contracted with another

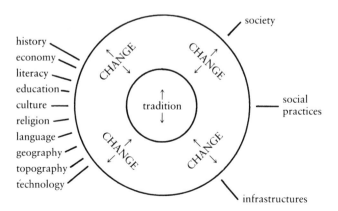

FIG. 3.1. Components of change.

producer of equipment, the cost of re-gearing for another system would make the present system obsolete.

In a similar position, Saudi Arabia installed enough telephone cable and switching systems to wire every home of the mountain city of Abha, but the Hyatt multinational hotel chain absorbed all existing telephone connections, leaving the people of the city without adequate telephone exchanges.

Technologies themselves exert certain influences and consequences for change. For example, the portability of ethnotronic technologies makes regulation more difficult. Black market and underground technologies and software are difficult to monitor from a governmental perspective; indeed, many "illicit" technologies and content exists in response to government policies, and therefore become a significant component of change, although it may not be easy to detect or track the number of technologies or the content of the software. In this case, projecting change becomes more speculative, but still an important component of the cultural context.

Theoretical Influences

Obviously, it has taken many years to get to the point of looking at change as organic, rather than as a linear "progressive," or even positive experience. In the West, we have been dominated by a number of theories throughout the 1900s that supported modernization or change due to technological availability.

Some of the theories that have contributed to an understanding of change as a component of social development grew out of the availability and presence of new technologies. A theoretical forerunner of the notion of change as an important component of "development," came from the work of William Ogburn (1927) who authored the theory of "culture lag." Ogburn's idea was that any new technological form (in those days, primarily telephones or automobiles) would cause a rift in society because there would always be those who could purchase these luxuries, and those who could not. Some people would always lag behind others when it came to innovations.

Ogburn's work emanated from the University of Chicago and the "Chicago School" of social inquiry. Scholars such as Robert Park, Ernest W. Burgess, John Dewey, George H. Mead, and Harold Lasswell had introduced scientific analysis of social issues through collaborative investigations that raised several new questions about society, culture, and the study of related issues. Many of the methods employed by those scholars gave rise to social science and a decidedly determinist viewpoint stating that any scientific methodology would yield results rich in evaluative measure. Technology, as it was viewed, was considered "progressive," and therefore an agent of modernization, and the social study of modernization a valid topic for social inquiry.

Post World War II interest in "developing" nations became more prevalent in the academic world because, as Mowlana (1986) indicated "new methods of inquiry had been developed, an interest in these countries began to be cultivated because of emerging independence from colonial powers, and because technologies began to erase the distances among countries" (p. 19). In the context of a developing country, culture lag often is viewed first as a lag between the elites and the masses. This is often due to cost and access of the technologies in question; the demand for distribution systems, products, and infrastructures takes more time to establish, but if and when these problems are met, the emphasis falls on the individual who wishes to possess the technology. Therefore, three distinct lag periods are evident, but not commensurate in time or value.

Work habits, cultural practices, and values must match the technological context, or a type of social stress may be experienced. This may occur through an individual's resistance to technical change, or internalized social practices that posit alien personal values against the "techniques" provided by new technology.

According to the standard diffusion model, a technology is not diffused until it has been accepted. Cost, access to technology, and possession of technology may be impediments to the stage of acceptance. In most developing countries, pressure to innovate comes from the government and is integrally related to the policy dimensions. Sometimes pressure is exerted toward the government to modify policies for innovation. An example could be provided by the Indian government's decision to make color television available to people in urban centers, when formerly, black-and-white television had been available, but massive expenditures had been made toward getting television service to people in rural areas and the urban dwellers exerted pressure on the government to spend resource money for a technical upgrade to color broadcasts for the more urban (and generally more affluent) viewers.

Innovation for social change often comes from the loudest voices of the population. These may represent legitimate concerns of the masses, or they may represent the most vocal interest groups. An example from Argentina may be seen within the context of the many political parties who exert pressure on the dominant political party to act in ways which will mollify the most urgent concerns of the interest groups. Almost every party has a faction that subscribes to an *antidependentista* view, (antidependency, an emphasis on indigenous production of goods and services), or *dependentista* sentiment (an acknowledgment that aid and cooperation must come from outside of the impoverished nation).

A major influence in theoretical work addressing developing nations has been the theme of modernization that emerged after World War II. Tying economic development to social and technological development, modernization theorists sought to bring the quality of living up to the level of production through means of improving a nation's capacity to produce goods. Scholars worked with organizations such as the United Nations to evaluate communication potential within various developing countries with an eye to providing development aid for the foundations of infrastructures in radio and telephone that would aid science, education, and culture (UNESCO). Often the criteria used to measure development relied on the number of telephone receivers that could be made available to populations or some other such numerical evaluation.

The development of literacy skills were at one time considered a necessary thrust for developing nations, leading to studies that made several attempts to delineate generic prescriptions for modernization and development (and many of these experiments are still being conducted around the world). Among some of the earlier ones were findings such as those provided by Schramm and Ruggles (1967):

1. only after a country reaches 10% of urbanization does its literacy rate begin to rise significantly;
2. thereafter, urbanization and literacy increase together in a direct, monotonic relationship until they reach 25%;
3. once societies are about 25% urbanized, the highest correlation of media consumption is with literacy.

It may become apparent very quickly that measuring literacy may not have any impact at all on the types of new communication technologies that are becoming more prevalent in developing countries today. What is more, the measure of literacy must be read within a cultural context; in some societies the ability to read, or to read only specific types of texts is class or gender bound; in other languages (like Farsi or Arabic) the language is not easily recorded on paper, and the spoken word takes precedence over written records of materials.

Many of the statistics that reflect literacy levels are also somewhat problematic. There is no one definitive standard of literacy, and therefore nations may have varying approaches to documenting trends. For example, some nations measure literacy by the number of people who pass through formal education, whereas others count the literate population by those who purchase newspapers or magazines. In some nations, literacy of the formal languages only are counted, whereas literacy in a native language is overlooked. Finally, there is always the problem of whether literacy measures the ability to read, or comprehension of materials. Even the industrialized nations have several reports based on different scales and measurements that obfuscate what literacy is, and how much exists.

In the 1960s, questions of the dominant paradigm began to arise from a variety of Western viewpoints. Canadians like Harold Innis and Marshall McLuhan began to focus on the questions of technology as mediators of a different sort that had inherent characteristics that also influenced users' behaviors and challenged the notion that content and form of media could be treated as separate issues.

European traditions began to effect the study of the relationship of content and technological form as French intellectuals entered the "dispersion age" with Pierre Bordieu and Claude Passeron questioning the existence of a sociology of mass media ("Massmediology"). Jacques Ellul questioned "technique" necessary to engage in forms of technology, suggesting that technology itself can never be neutral—but that every form of technology exerts a certain way of doing things that influences human's perception of that technological form and its use.

In the United States, Tichenor, Olien, and Donohue (1970) introduced the idea of "knowledge gap" based on the belief that the more education increases levels of gaps among subgroups in a society. Similar to Ogburn's theory, the "knowledge gap" suggested differential growth.

In 1976, Rogers published a major article on the "Passing of the Dominant Paradigm (1976)." His work evaluated the growth of the avenues of inquiry into development studies, and called for a reassessment of outmoded notions of development that could be measured by the counting of instruments or the notion that modernization (including literacy) was necessary for development. In later studies, Rogers developed his new theoretical base by incorporating more emphasis on the developing nations' social structure, investigation of individual participation, and networking to look at problem-oriented situations.

THE INNOVATION PROCESS AND DIFFUSION RESEARCH

We discussed the concept of the diffusion of innovations briefly in chapter 2, but we would like to elaborate on that theory at this point by addressing further work in the area. Katz, Lewin, and Hamilton (1963) suggested that any diffusion model includes:

1. acceptance
2. over time
3. of some specific item—an idea or practice
4. by individuals, groups or other adopting units, linked to
5. specific channels of communication,

6. to a social system, and

7. to a given system of values, or culture.

The diffusion model has been used for studies from various perspectives, among which are economic studies, new product developments, and the impact on old and new industries affected through change (Rogers, 1976b; Rosegger, 1976).

From a development perspective, the diffusion of technologies and technological change suggest configurations of questions including marketing, policy, control, sociocultural impact, the effect on educational patterns, government philosophy (policy), and social practice. Along with notions of a new, first-time technology entering the culture, as in the case of a unique medium such as television, the demand for peripheral technologies and enhanced technologies can also begin to grow. Using television as the example, it is possible to discuss the use of videocassette players and tapes, black-and-white versus color systems, computerization, and enhanced systems of high-definition TV (HDTV) and digitalization. Another example would be obvious in charting the growth from a typewriter to a word processor, personal computer, interactive system, and so on.

In addition to a technological diffusion, the diffusion of social practices is a complementary issue. Rosegger (1976) has written that the role of *information flows* and the concept of *resistance* is of paramount importance in diffusion research. How information about a technology and its capacity reaches the individual, and the credibility and accountability of the source of the information, influences the rate of adoption. If there is resistance to the technology or its use, it may not always be uniform resistance. Likewise, when we demand an updated technology, the old technology is not abandoned, but rather integrated further into existing social practices.

New Information and Communication Order

A milestone in theoretical development occurred as the Third World nations called for the New World Information Order (NWIO). In their voicing of the need for what would be considered a more "balanced flow" of information, the concerns of developing countries became more important, and more obvious. We are more concerned about the technology needs of nations in the NWIO. The universal system of HDTV would encourage a balanced flow; likewise, technological changes could facilitate greater access to low-cost systems and compatible software.

Access to satellite communications by all nations is another major point. When distribution channels are limited, the potential for the diffusion of innovations, social practices, and effective policies for technological application are curtailed and the adoption process becomes moot.

The transfer of technology discussed in chapter 1 has further ramifications in creating a free and balanced flow of information. Particularly when married to the idea that technical expertise and training can flow from one country to another, a more level playing field for information exchange can become more of a reality. Thus, technical cooperation may involve the exchange of skills and expertise, as well as technology transfer and the creation of intellectual and technical strengths that may increase indigenous production.

Cultural Domination.   An important criticism and consideration for areas of technology transfer, content exchange, and expert training in technological systems and design is that of cultural domination. In this concept the host (producing) nation exports more than technology, software, or instruction. Along with the exchange comes the dominant ideology of the producing nation that affects the cultural context of the developing nation by infusing alien concepts into the traditional culture.

Cultural domination can take place through imposition of "experts" who are put in charge of (usually) lower paid, indigenous workers and the types of social technologies that come from these organizational components. The indigenization of technologies, content, or control of information seldom occurs in places where technologies and systems of implementation are purchased through private means or through bi- or multilateral agreements. In these cases, the "wheel of change" is shaped (or distorted) further because of foreign intervention.

Social Technology Models.   Social technologies rely on shared systems of beliefs, practices, and values. Two notions posit opposite ends of the continuum on individual's predilections for using technologies. The first is commonly called *technological determinism,* which suggests that technology itself becomes the motivating force for other resultant changes throughout society. The other has been termed *technological liberalism,* which posits a notion that the primary effect of technology is moral, uplifting, and inherently good. To simplify the differences, it could be said that technological determinism is a process of fate, whereas technological liberalism is a process of choice. Of course complexities arise by the levels of individual ascription to the measures of these terms. However, each can be reduced to a concept that carries great communicative weight in perpetuating notions that impinge on innovation, adoption, and use.

Mobilization of individuals is something that is often difficult to force or determine in developing nations because of the relationship of individuals to their classes, social systems, and societies. As a result, the most effective movements for change toward prosocial goals in developing nations most often comes from a recognition of the importance of grassroot movements (Basu, 1987; Mainwaring, 1987; Narula, 1990).

Who might become an opinion leader within a society is often difficult to predict, particularly if a researcher is not familiar with local customs and traditions. Often gender biases and sexual roles play a significant part of social technologies in developing nations because men and women often are not encouraged to communicate with the opposite sex outside of the home. These types of constraints also require different generative mechanisms for the diffusion of innovations, ideas, and motivation for change. Added to this, is the gender inequities that often disregard the work of women because it cannot be easily quantified within the traditional GNP figures, (Bernard, 1987) and the reality that the majority of the population of the Third World today is under the age of 15. These extreme cases of gender and age differentiations place even more social stress on the communicative patterns of people within society, and again, call policies toward *change* into question.

Similarly, the relationship of the government with the individuals and masses suggest special ways that determine access to policymakers and their willingness to listen to others. Often quasi-governmental organizations blur the boundaries and are therefore somewhat circumspect by both masses and governmental elites. In many developing countries today, the greatest amount of money earmarked for experimentation and new technology development (particularly satellites and computers) falls to the defense organizations, who often work within bureaucracies that may not openly share information with the public. In this way, governments make huge expenditures toward facilities that then become the standards or templates for further development in the private and public sectors.

Finally, the concept of *selective exposure* is extremely important as we look toward an information society. Human beings tend to seek reduction of any possible imbalance brought about by change, through seeking information that is compatible with preconceived notions. Social technologies then, also address the issues of gender, education, occupation, and social class in understanding how people organize their surroundings in ways that ease transitions from one lifestyle to another.

The challenges of integrating technology and culture might be more specifically identified in Table 3.1.

Within this framework, each nation might identify specific goals and challenges provided by hardware and software systems.

ADVANCED TECHNOLOGICAL SYSTEMS

The international community is concerned with two major aspects of development; worldwide flow and exchange of human and economic resources, and identifying the markets for distribution and exchange of information, entertainment, and technology. In almost every case, the advanced techno-

TABLE 3.1
Communication Technology Determinants

Culture Specific	1. Culture Determinants	Creation of Social Technology
Communication Forms	• cultural values of elites and masses	
Communication Acts	• superimposed societal values • media structures, controls, and practices • work ethics, organizational practices	
	2. Five Value Assumptions	Developing Social Competence
	• regard for human nature • relationship of human to nature • orientation toward activity • time orientation • types of relations among people	
	3. Cultural Resources	Putting Cultural Resources at Risk
	• language, religion, ideology • values, ways of doing and making things • myths, stories, artifacts • typifications, interpretive procedures	
	4. Acceptance of Technology	Culture-lag
	• 1,2,3 are accepted	

logical systems borrow conceptually from those technological systems that preceded them; the tendency to want to build on old concepts is strong although it may not be possible. In the following sections we discuss the trends in technological systems.

Television Broadcasting

A 1972–1973 UNESCO study (Varis, 1983) found that at that time there was an overwhelming one-way flow of television programs and news from the industrialized countries to the others. In 1983, a similar study showed that there was no major change in this one-way flow, but that there were additional trends toward regional exchanges of materials, and that privately owned and commercial satellite dishes connected to cable systems have spread over much of Latin America and the Caribbean (Libby, 1988).

Throughout the 1980s there has been a sharp rise in the number of television channels available to people in many countries, partly because of the growing trends of privatization of media within nations, and also due to the geographic distribution of countries which facilitates receiving signals broadcast from one country in another. Also, satellites, cable, and distribution forms of media through videocassettes have increased distribution of content. Similarly, the technologies of television reception have continued to decrease in cost and become more portable through miniaturization.

The current concern over a possible worldwide technical standard for the emerging technology of HDTV has tremendous potential to foster international program distribution. Certainly, one of the most obvious criticisms of such a program would include the capacity to broadcast entertainment programs, laden with foreign cultural content, to audiences unaware of the social dynamics at play in the program production, distribution, and use in the host countries, but the opposing issues lead us to believe that educational programming could also be distributed at reduced cost.

Three competing systems are presently under consideration by individual industrialized nations and consortia; the United States has proposed an HDTV technical standard of 1,050 lines per second; the Japanese, 1,125 lines per second, and the European community, 1,250 lines per second. All of the systems proposed would increase the aspect ratio of the television receiver from 4:3 to 5:3, and even the U.S. system of least resolution would approximate the picture quality of 35mm film (see Fig. 3.2).

Like noncompatible systems of television currently available throughout the world, the competition for HDTV also concerns itself with the noncompatibility issues, as well as signal distribution. The Japanese system proposes

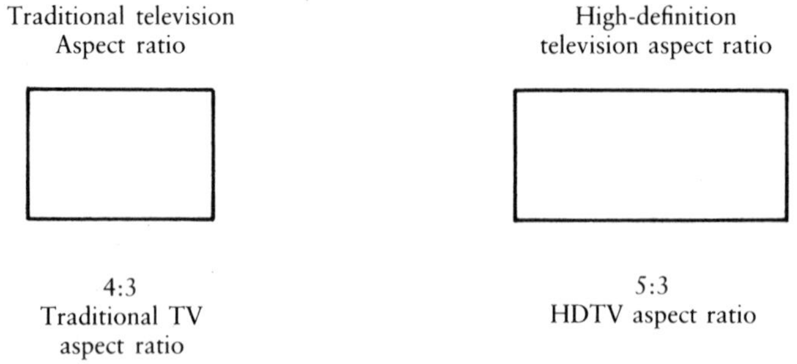

Traditional television Aspect ratio	High-definition television aspect ratio
4:3 Traditional TV aspect ratio	5:3 HDTV aspect ratio

FIG. 3.2. Aspect ratio of traditional verse HDTV.

a digital transmission of information, whereas the U.S. system would require twice the frequency size to simultaneously send two signal carriers. Each system has its benefits and drawbacks, but they all suggest that unless a system decoder could be developed to modify existing receivers, old television sets could become obsolete, unless international agreements foster an arrangement by which old signal distribution will remain while HDTV becomes a technology for international diffusion. At any rate, the problems for the potential use of HDTV currently deal with national and intranational discussions on technical standards and receiver compatibility, and most probably will not be a major force in global broadcasting until the late 1990s.

The Video Boom

There are currently four "video rich" areas of the world: Japan and South-East Asia, the Arab countries, Western Europe, and North America. Within these regions, both the use of video and the size of the markets have provided distribution systems that facilitate many uses. As with all systems of hardware and software, there are both benefits and drawbacks for users and distributors.

While videocassettes in Western Europe and North America are most heavily used for time-shifting of broadcast television and for playing prerecorded entertainment or self-help features, the nations of the Third World have extended their use for maintaining cultural links with home cultures. Migrant communities in various countries may watch feature films in their own language and feel more connected with their own societies. A popular use of religious videotapes has allowed individuals to follow their own religious ceremonies even though they may be too far from their point of origin.

Following the same principles, however, it is possible to see that the individual audiences and distribution systems of videocassettes have also brought about problems, such as video piracy, copyright and royalty payments, and materials that governments may not approve of, such as pornography, advertising, or underground materials.

Almost every country that has access to videocassettes, however, has used these distribution forms to aid in both formal and nonformal education, for political messages, and for basic information (such as railway information or traffic protocols). Although the industrialized nations generally have central facilities for distribution of cassettes, many Third World nations rely on informal distribution (legal or illegal), or on systems such as mobile video parlors (similar to mobile cinemas) to make the viewing of these tapes possible to people who may not have their own videocassette players.

Satellites

A technology that would further enhance the utility of HDTV already in existence is the tremendous capacity for satellite distribution. Whether through direct broadcast satellite or by linking satellite distribution to terrestrial relays, as is presently done, the satellite's capacity to transfer information has become one of the most potentially exciting tools for program distribution and information sharing for industrialized nations as well as for nations with limited resources and geographic problems.

Projects that have utilized satellite communications are INSAT (a project of India, discussed in chapter 4); the Canadian ANIK system, used to reach the indigenous population centered to the northern most sections of the country; the PEACESAT system that facilitated interaction and program sharing among nations of the South Pacific; and the ARABSAT system, linking the various Arab nations.

As a distribution system, satellites provide tremendous capacity for a variety of uses, if a nation has access to the satellite system, including the technological knowledge to best use the resource.

Digitalization

Digitalization is another technological possibility that offers a universal system that can be distributed via satellite, or wired communication (particularly through fiber optics). Digitalization of information makes the same channels of communication more useful by piggybacking or doubling up on the amount of information that is carried through traditional conduits. Some of the benefits of digitalization of information include cheaper means of distribution (once the infrastructure has been converted to be compatible with digital information), the potential for more standardized technologies, and greater information exchange. The most significant negative effect would be the replacement of old infrastructures to accommodate the high-speed, information-laden channels. For many developing nations that suffer from inadequate or worn-out infrastructures, the initial cost investment of digital technologies may well provide a large step into a more information-reliant society. In some ways, developing nations may use digital technologies faster and more efficiently than industrialized nations that have workable infrastructures, and that may have a longer change-over time toward advanced digitalization. Certainly fiber optics would increase the potential for digital technologies to be used. A fiber optic carries significantly more information than traditional co-axial cable, such as that commonly used for telephones or cable television. Generations of fiber optics have different capacities, but a general agreement is that one fiber optic system can carry more than ninety times that of a traditional co-axial cable. The fiber optics in development now could carry significantly more information than that. Other benefits include the flexibility and durability of fiber compared to cable, and the relative low cost of the raw material (silicon, vs. copper). For nations seeking to increase wired systems, like terrestrial telephony, fiber optics will enhance the capacity for information exchange.

Computerization and Data Transfer

The electronic processing and digitalization in the print media have stimulated two complementary trends; a modularization of the various printing processes, and a rationalization of the modular processes into an integrated system. This has led to the computerization of all steps in the preparation of text and graphics, improvements in control, and direct printing by laser that produces both text and images.

Electronic desktop publishing using a laser printer is sufficient for most pre-printing needs of in-house and small community newspapers, and offers myriad possibilities for updating material that changes rapidly. In many countries where paper is costly and difficult to obtain, or where the production of academic books is restricted, desktop publishing may provide a relatively low-cost alternative to traditional modes of information production.

Transborder Data Flow

The information intensive industries such as banking, insurance, airlines, and other international business heavily depend on the transmission of data around the world. The statistics however, are difficult to obtain because this type of information cannot be correlated with other indices such as distribution of computers, increased telecommunication services, or rapid development of software services. Unless the material is monitored as it is processed, transmitted or stored, we cannot have an accurate gauge of how much material crosses national borders each day.

SITUATIONS AND CONTEXTS: MEETING CULTURAL
CHALLENGES THROUGH ADVANCED TECHNOLOGIES

Programs in Distance Education

Despite political and infrastructural problems, the notion of using media as a distribution agent for educational purposes has become an important option for many nations experiencing geographical problems, large rural populations, and a lack of trained teachers. Many experimental programs have been funded by agencies like the United Nations, the World Bank, and others to explore the capacity for using more advanced technologies for educational purposes. Generally, using distance education programs finds favor among a variety of individuals in many classes, based on the altruistic use of the technology, and the all-too-common problems of educating individuals in remote regions, without adequate teachers or resources.

For example, in rural areas of India, all types of nontraditional technologies have been earmarked for educational purposes. The realities of the potential for media such as audio and videocassettes, pre-programmed tapes in the nonbroadcast mode, and teacher supplementation technologies and software have been given priority, despite the difficulties of costs. An unwillingness by some teachers to travel to rural areas is a reality that influences the government's commitment to education for the masses.

Distance education programs enhances not only the quality, but even more so, the quantity of education programs available to a population. All ages can be served; ideas can be suggested in a more timely, and also, often a more culturally relevant context. For example, language differences, social practices, and religious beliefs can be more clearly articulated by designing messages for specific audiences.

Audiocassettes

Features of audiocassettes that have revolutionized a certain corner of the media market include the low-cost, reusability, and portability of this form of software. As a result, audiocassettes can easily be smuggled, duplicated, or erased when necessary. Although surprisingly little has been written on the use of audiocassettes in developing nations, there is evidence to indicate that these small objects have been used extensively to create change by political means in many countries. Several specific examples are discussed in later chapters, but we should point out that although many cassettes are openly sold in some markets, the pirating of entertainment cassettes has created several problems for cultural sovereignty, laws on content, and most importantly on the global level, international copyright standards.

Health and Education. Audiocassettes, videocassettes, and other software has been used in many countries to extend health and education to people in rural areas. The relative low cost of these distribution forms is a special feature for their use. Literacy is also not a problem when the means of distribution of messages comes from an audio or visual medium.

In urban areas, displays can be set up to offer specialized information and educational tips in hospitals, clinics, and other social agencies. Advanced telephone systems rely on audiocassettes for special information accessed by a caller, with one individual to plug in information tapes to specifically address the caller's informational needs. Obviously, one of the best uses for audiocassettes concerns information for the handicapped, particularly the blind.

Tourism. Several Third World nations have developed tourism as a partial answer to bringing in money from outside the country. In recent years, Asian nations in particular have begun to feel the benefits of allowing contact with the outside world as increased travel opportunities bring not only businesses but individuals to these regions. Tourism programs on video- or audiotape help visitors to determine what packaged tours to take, where to go, and even, in some cases, where to stay.

National tourism programs have begun to link hotels, rail systems, and airline information through computer networks to facilitate communication for travelers to these regions, and in some cases, these needs have called for the financial underwriting of enhanced communication systems for use primarily by business and government, but sometimes, with benefits to the local populations as well.

Illicit Activity and Power. The major problem with the distribution systems and enhanced uses of technology hardware and software as mentioned earlier, concerns the possibility for illegal activity. Because so many of today's information technologies are small and portable, traditional means of assessing their presence (legal or illegal) within a country has become a subject of speculation. Sales figures may indicate how many technologies have been legally purchased within a country, and by whom, but the flow of illegal technology and software is very difficult to monitor.

Many technologies and software systems come from migrant workers who return home with presents, goods, and belongings they have obtained elsewhere. Sometimes the technological system purchased in one country is not compatible with the technological systems within the home country, and can only be run with software also brought in from outside.

Because these technologies and software systems are so easily moved across borders, governments are often at a loss to know what to do about them. In many cases these artifacts are challenging traditional laws of ownership, censorship, and public information. Although it is difficult to discuss these topics in general, it would be sufficient to say that in many cases the technologies that do not rely on large-scale infrastructural developments may perhaps have the greatest potential for creating change within any country.

Cultural Challenges

At the international level, IT is transferred (through technical expertise and technology transfer), and develops markets within developing countries. Within all of these components, there is the possibility for creating dependency or for enhancing market opportunities.

Within this model, it is possible to see how the policies that influence technological development, also affect foreign policy, reinforce economic power and domination, and maintain defense power. The result then, is a maintenance of power by the constant reinforcement of social support.

Information technology models in industrialized nations reflect those nations' ideologies that support the development of labor saving devices for effective use of human resources and time. Market forces of of industrialized nations (particularly under capitalism) proceeds through a series of technical innovation, experimentation with content, and finally, regulation (or the policy stage).

SUMMARY

As evidenced by the examples in this chapter, media technologies and social technologies work hand in hand. The target is to reach the appropriate balance—but sometimes the equilibrium is disturbed due to innovation pressure.

Technologies themselves have characteristics that influence the level and amount of change within nations. Legal and illegal market forces contribute to a changing environment, even though the changes may be more difficult to relate to the specific technologies or software. When this happens, speculation complicates both government and the masses actions, and further obfuscates the social/technological relationship and impact.

India: A Case Study

With time as the most scarce resource for a developing country and distance as the most formidable constraint for vast masses in the diffused sector, countries like India may find in the new communication modes wisely blended with the traditional modes . . . corresponding to the Gandhi-Nehru vision of technology with a human face.
—P. C. Joshi, Chairman, Indian Institute of Mass Communication
(1988)

India is heading for the 21st century with a technological model for development. To accomplish this, the government has decided to concentrate on "development phases" to encourage the use of science and technology within the nation. India has decided to focus attention toward five particular communication technologies/systems to serve the needs and interests of the greatest number of people. With problems of distance, cultures, languages, and beliefs that cannot be served by one mass message through one communication medium, this nation has developed a system of grassroot mobilization toward the use of new communication technologies.

HISTORY

India's subservience as a colony to Britain, the enormous population spread inequitably among the country; the varieties of languages, castes, cultures, religions; and the vast land mass have all posed development problems for the nation. Although traditions of radio, telephony, and television have all been present within some parts of the society, each of the traditional media have emerged amid controversy and specific cultural challenges.

For example, the British brought private clubs to India as early as 1924, and shortly thereafter a private organization, the Indian Broadcasting Company (IBC) set up facilities in Calcutta and Bombay, only to be dissolved in 1930 because of financial difficulties (Lent, 1988). By 1936 a radio corporation was set up along the model of the BBC and was given the name of All India Radio (AIR). The programming, however, was slanted toward British interests and therefore (especially during WWII) Indian listeners were highly skeptical of the purpose and programming available. Television was set up on an experimental basis in Delhi by 1959, also under AIR, but in 1976 the organization was split so that Doordarshan Television accommodated the television programming services, and Akashvani Radio, the radio services. Over the years, the radio services began to become more credible sources of information, particularly among the 90% illiterate population.

Like telephone service, the early television services reached a small percentage of the population until 1982, when INSAT-1A, India's first satellite was made operational. Within 2 years additional transmitters were introduced, color television became a viability for urban areas, and a national network for simultaneous relay, including microwave links were established throughout the country. By 1984, the government added a second television channel to specifically aim at regional and local interests (Lent, 1988). These changes occurred as part of the government's plan to increase telecommunications facilities throughout the country.

The urban telephone system also started in some areas on a small-scale basis in the 1950s, but even at that time the system was small, inefficient, and unable to support growth. Telephone concentration was in urban areas and there were no thoughts about extending telephony services to rural areas—a problem that has continued for the government and masses perspectives today.

Prior to taking an active approach to coordinating technological and social policies, the government had ambivalent attitudes and policies toward importing appropriate technologies as well as issues of the transfer of technologies. Like many developing nations, India has had past policies of not importing and transferring technologies that has restricted the acceleration of participation in the information society. The government has moved slowly and cautiously because only an integrated system of plans for economic, technological, and social change was considered viable.

Since independence in 1947, the Indian government has instituted a series of development plans that articulate the rationale, objectives, and means of development to be achieved during specific time periods. Although a discussion of these goals and the conceded necessity of the role of communication would take far too many pages to cover adequately in this chapter, the national goals and role of communication have been abstracted and outlined in Table 4.1.

India's focus on technolɾgy is not so much because of political considerations but more from a social development perspective. Politically, India is a guided democracy but essentially a social welfare state. Therefore, the major focus is the social welfare of the majority of its population by improving quality of life for them whether by social, economic, or technological means. The political will of the ruling party plays a significant role as to which of these means are adopted and to what extent.

The 1980s was the start of the technology decade in India even though many forms of distribution have been available since the 1970s. Changes to policies in the 1980s began to focus on the following:

1. revitalizing current technologies for a move to more advanced technologies;

2. a movement away from idea that technology is for the elite, and a greater emphasis on grassroot diffusion; and

3. the role of technology to improve the quality of life through well-planned "technology missions" (high-priority areas, such as water, sanitation, health immunization, literacy).

The technology model is unique from many other developing nations because of the social considerations and priorities given to mission areas. These social considerations determine the technology issues, priorities, policies, and the perspectives of the government and masses.

The government perspective in this case study describes the technology missions to be achieved, and the significance of the political input in formulating social policies rather than political policies for technology development and application. The masses perspective describes the will of the people for technology acceptance and various technological challenges that they face.

The net achievement will be how well the political will and the will of the masses is coordinated. India's information model described in the case study is based on three social principles described by Pitroda (1987):

1. *Connectivity:* Everybody needs to be connected to the whole nation for communication, whether it is by telephone or by interactive computer terminal. Because of the distribution of the population, rural connectivity is most important.

2. *Access to information:* Information must be shared without any distinction of socioeconomic status or caste. The problems of social, economic, and technical access are interrelated with the government's

TABLE 4.1
Development Decades and National Plans in India

Decade	5-Year National Plan
1950–1960	1951–1956; adoptive-administrative phase of community development *Role of Communication*—to educate and inform people; also to motivate them and secure their participation in the growth process 1956–1961; development of the integrative-technical phase; and democratic decentralization *Role of Communication*—to help participatory communication for self-help and self reliance rather than creating a dependency on the government
1960–1970	1961–1966; to secure an increase in the national income by 5% per annum; and ensure a pattern of investment to sustain this growth; also to attain self-sufficiency in food grains and increase food production to meet requirements of industry and export; also to expand basic industries (i.e., steel, chemical, fuel, and power for 10-year growth in industrialization *Role of Communication*—to strengthen public cooperation and participation by intensifying publicity for implications of rapid development throughout the country
1970–1980	1969–1974; to raise the standard of living by programs to promote equality and social justice, emphasize improving conditions of less privileged and weaker sections of society through education and employment, reduction of concentration of wealth, income and economic power, and aim at an annual compound rate of growth in the net domestic product of 5.7% *Role of Communication*—to inform, educate and motivate masses for adoption of these development programs. 1974–1978; to achieve economic self-reliance; raise consumption standards of people living below poverty line; give high priority for controlling inflation and achieving stability; to achieve targeted annual growth rates of 5.5% in national income *Role of Communication*—to change attitudes toward the acceptance of development programs
1980–1990	1980–1985; to achieve economic and technological self-reliance; improve the quality of life for economically and socially handicaped people through a Basic Minimum Needs program; reduce poverty; strengthen redistribution biases in public policies to favor the poor; reduce regional inequalities in the pace of development; promote active involvement of all sections of the society in the process of development through education, communication and institutional strategies. *Role of Communication* to develop community resources by educating masses for community identity

Source: Abstracted from Narula (1984).

goal to provide access to an optimum number of people, but if the technology is unaffordable it becomes a constraint.

3. *Reliability:* An integrated telecommunication national network providing connectivity to everbody must be a reliable system.

4. *Acceptability:* Information technology has to be applied and linked to peoples' lifestyles.

5. *National focus:* An integrated network that is accessible and reliable allows connectivity to all groups of people.

The Government Perspective

The goal throughout the 1980s was to foster India's participation in the communication revolution by concentrating on the five major communication technologies of television, satellites, video, computers, and the enhancement of telecommunication systems. The Indian government has also determined that a major factor in enhancing NCTs is the number of people who would benefit from technological adoption. To these ends the facilitation of communication by the masses has required that decisions be made that would convey the optimum information to the population, and that it be both physically and financially accessible to the masses. To do this, the NCTs are being delivered to the masses within the contexts of their own lifestyles and social systems.

The following issues have been determined to best serve the governmental goals for the integration of NCTs:

1. the development of social technologies and the soft infrastructure to accept the hardware;

2. manufacturing the indigenous hardware so that it is cost effective as well and is able to meet the indigenous needs of the people;

3. encouraging advanced technologies and not concentrating on basic or scratch technologies; and

4. encouraging the development of first-level technology in certain key areas and "sky-level" technology in the long-range planning stages to develop technological capabilities.

In India, information technology presents a generation gap. The decision makers and policymakers now think in terms of the 21st century, but when it comes to applied technology for the masses, only 15th century technology is used. Because India is not a commercial society, the technological imperatives have been traditionally slow to develop, but the capacities of the NCTs indicate that change may be coming fast.

Some government policymakers now are beginning to understand that efficient telecommunications are critical for moving the economy and that NCTs can be integrated through strategies for social and economic development. As part of the integrated approach, the country needs to be self-reliant, and must not become a "dumping ground" for other nations' obsolete technologies. Therefore, the government's perspective requires that NCTs are viewed within the Indian cultural ethos.

The Masses Perspective.   In the past, information in India has not been easily shared with the masses. It has been passed from the people to the elites, but filtering from top to bottom has been very slow and inefficient. Traditionally, 90% of the population of India has remained in the villages where there has been a low rate of literacy, mass poverty, and large-scale unemployment. A value system that has perpetuated a fatalism manifesting itself in people's passive acceptance of their circumstances and an attitude toward individual dependency has resulted in what UNESCO has called "exploitative linkages"—patterns of social relations in which the masses are regularly exploited by the local elites (Narula, 1984).

This has led to a masses perspective that approaches new technologies as something that government may plan to provide for them, but that those technologies should be easily available as well as accessible and cost effective with efficient and meaningful performance. Some members of the elite group have started to think that government industrial policies should allow them to choose some of the technologies that may be beneficial only to the few consumers but profit oriented, but concerns by other members of the population have dictated that the government will have control over its communication technology policies as guided by the aforementioned priorities.

It is interesting to note that "India's durable democratic traditions has created the political space in which social movements have flourished" (Basu, 1987, p. 647). Throughout the country, many grassroots organizations have facilitated issues concerning development. Basu described three special interest groups that have a variety of allegiances, but that all illustrate the cultural challenges acknowledged by village-level organizations, and that show the influences of Ghandhian philosophy, tribal cultural values, and Christian liberation theology. She concluded that the democratic system in India both fosters an interest in grassroots mobilization of interested parties, but that sometimes the structures of government also undermine the possibility of the masses and government working together in internal and external political environments.

INFORMATION TECHNOLOGIES

Telephony and Telecommunications

Although India is proud to be one of the first countries to introduce the telephone shortly after its invention, the more than 100-year-old tradition is badly in need of upgrading and modernization. The country's development of a telecommunications infrastructure is similar to France, where even in 1960 the system was reckoned as one of the worst in Europe. Only by a government committed to improvement like the French government, can a poor system be revitalized into one of the best in the region within a relatively few years. Robert J. Saunders (1986), co-author of a World Bank Publication, *Telecommunications and Economic Development,* has opined that under-investment is one of the factors responsible for the poor telephone system in India that hampers India's development process. Because telecommunication in India is a commercial enterprise, resources are not the real problems. A clear goal and will are the basic issues.

In earlier days, the Indian telephone system was run by the government to serve the needs of a small clientele. In the last 20 years or so there has been structural change in the economy that has also called for new management systems. A commercial service cannot operate efficiently in the form of a government department. This is a lesson that the public has learned all over the world. In countries where privatization is not favored, the compromise formula is to convert it into an autonomous corporation subject to parliament directives. Such a setup ensures flexibility of a commercial organization and responsiveness to democratic urges and parliamentary control.

In the mid-1980s, a very low telephone density prevailed in the country— only 4 telephones per 1,000. What led to the telecommunication mess was an emphasis of borrowed technology, technological transplant, centralized organization, and lack of national commitment of failure to develop human resources. However, as the country entered the latter half of the 1980s, the improvements have enhanced function and performance.

The revitalization has been made possible by updating technology expansion, using computerization, enhancing rural communication, and introducing new features. The organizations involved are both public and private, such as the Department of Electronics (DOT), the Telecommunication Research Center (TRC), the Center for Development of Technology (C.DOT), and the Indian Telephone Institute (ITI). Except for C.DOT all are in the public sector.

What is still needed is an integrated telecommunication network to make use of powerline transmission, radio systems, and fiber optics. These communication systems are required to support speech, telemetry, telesignalling, teleprinting, telecontrol, teleprotection, and facsimile transmission. The Power Line Carrier Communication system (PLCC) has been one of the most common and popular facilities used for this purpose, but it alone is not adequate for the potential volume of traffic, so co-axial cable and radio systems are presently being used.

The present trend is toward use of digital systems instead of prevalent analog systems to handle heavy telephone traffic. Digital systems offer highly improved systems, efficiency, and quality. The government is looking for both indigenous and imported technology in this context, and both private and public sectors are assigned this task. The digital systems are being imported from France and the digital electronic process control instruments are being manufactured with Japanese collaboration.

At present the efforts are to import and transfer the updated telecommunication technology so that telecommunication systems function efficiently through fiber optics for telephone cables, telephone instruments, or computerization of telephone instruments or telephone operations. There is currently a concentration on indigenous production and also on transfer of technology with major efforts to concentrate on the domestic front, and a likelihood that by 1995 such technology may be exported to other developing countries.

The expansion of government-established telecommunication research centers coincides with the entire telecommunication system switching over from analog to the modern digital electronic system during the seventh plan (1986–1991). The shift to a digital system would make the transmission more reliable and versatile, and would enable the telecommunication system to introduce the addition to voice data and facsimile or picture transmission services through telephone lines using the models developed by the research centers. Even computers could be interconnected over a long distance using telephone lines.

The telecom system is also introducing optical fibers for intercity connections, with Bombay and New Bombay to first be connected through optical fiber cables manufactured in India by the Hindustan Cables during the seventh plan.

A feature of the change that is being introduced in the telecom system is its increasing reliance on microprocessor-based equipment to speed up communications. With the telecom system increasingly restoring to satellite-based circuits for intercity connections, for data and facsimile transmission, and for other services, a whole range of equipment for this satellite-based transmission and for other services are also being developed.

The World Bank announced a $45 million loan to revitalize the telephone system in four major cities of India—New Delhi, Calcutta, Bombay, and Madras. The World Bank felt that telephone systems were seriously deficient in India and improved telecommunications are vital to market-oriented liberalization policies. The other organizations funding the project are the United Nations Development Plan (UNDP) and overseas credit funds of Japan. The project will help finance new digital transmission and switching facilities to increase telephone capacities in the four cities. It will also modernize and expand communication and satellite ground station networks, and set up a long distance management system to locate bypass or to eliminate bottlenecks in the phone network.

So far in India the main concentration of the telecommunication network is in urban areas only, but the costs are still prohibitive. There are no rural telephones. India has taken indigenous production of rural automatic exchanges (RAX). An experiment in one rural area that measured the effectiveness of the RAX was conducted in 1987, and found to be effective. The experiment showed that the technology was effective, but the costs of the services and receivers would still prohibit the individuals in the rural environment to have more than one telephone available for the village. This, however, would not support the RAX financial investment. The solution for the government is to either have one telephone in the village and not invest in the RAX, or, invest in the RAX and make the services inexpensive enough so that the people in the village can afford it.

These exchanges are designed by a private Indian organization C.DOT. RAX designed by C.DOT are not only cheap, but more compact, use less electric power than the imported ones, and are more suited to the Indian traffic conditions. The experimental Indian RAX is the first digital system that functions without air conditioning facilities. The second phase of the RAX project will concentrate on enhancing product features and capabilities. RAX aims at proper connectivity to 1 billion people and aims at 30 million phones against 3 million in rural areas.

Rural telephones are not only basic but a vital necessity in India. According to a study of UN telecommunication unions and an OECD study in Andhra rural region showed that even the poor people are willing to pay a large portion of their income for telephone use; otherwise they would have to carry the message by bus in person thus losing several day's wages or by sending a letter, which would mean a delay of days. Villagers would use the phone in emergencies and to convey urgent messages. The villagers' biggest complaint about the telephones is their unreliability and not their expense.

Computerization of the telephone network will enhance efficiency, and the government plans to computerize 26 medium-sized exchanges between 1987–1989. Already, computerization of trunk calls booked by the subscribers have been switched from manual handling to an automated system. In the computerized paperless exchanges the booked calls are arranged destination-wise, priority-wise, and according to the time of booking. The advantage of the system would be efficient handling of the booked calls and no call that is not booked through the operator or entered into the system will mature. The telecom target for the seventh plan (1987–1992) is to reach 24 million lines. The public sector Indian telephone industries plan to achieve these objectives by indigenous production, which includes 7 electronic switching systems (ESS), 20 lakhs (100,000) electronic push button telephones using the state of art technology, and to increase production of rotary dial telephones. It proposes to increase its digital trunk automatic exchange equipment (DTAX) capacity to 2.4 lakhs (see Table 4.2).

The other projects that are likely to be completed during the eighth national development plan are conventional communication systems like a cellular mobile system, TV microwave links, satellite communication equipment using a digital optical fiber system, small capacity multiplexing systems, wavelength multiplexed, and a high speed fiber-optic system.

The telecommunication policy of the government of India operates through the DOT. It has been wavering among allowing imports, indigenous production, and transfer of technology, but the DOT's emphasis is on self-reliance and indigenous production while at the same time, allowing imports of technology for C.DOT on the argument that it should imported until domestic production is fully possible.

The continuing failure of the DOT to evolve an effective perspective plan—not just data or information inputs but a backbone network for cities, towns and villages for at least 5 years at a time has created problems of planning, production, and expansion and of deciding technological feasibil-

TABLE 4.2
Information Technology Capacity in India

	1986	1990	2000
Telephone connections	3.16 million	4.5 million	19 million
Subscribers awaiting telephones	1 million	1.5 million	Nil
Telex connections	32,000	43,000	200,000
Villages with public phones or exchanges	32,000	43,000	600,000
Public call offices in cities/towns	20,000	35,000	1 million
Voice/data in business/ industry	negligible	10,000	800,000

25% of the urban population has 90% of all telephones
less than 6% of 575,000 village have public telephones
Of 3,000 cities, 400 have international STD facilities
There are 33 earth satellite stations providing 4,000 trunk circuits

Source: Telecom Mission Draft Report, (1987) Department of Telecommunications, New Delhi.

ity, retaining or redevelopment of the labor force. It is also unjustified to compare indigenous product price and that of the foreign equipment.

New Features in the Telephone System. New features are being introduced in the system gradually to update it and to make it more efficient through direct dialing on the national and international levels. Push button telephones are being provided to the upper level bureaucrats. Cellular mobile radio telephones are now available in the two metropolitan cities of Bombay and Delhi. To facilitate their interface, a convenient handbag-size cordless telephone instrument is being developed, and a radio base station is being set up at 10 km to ensure satisfactory performance. The new cellular phone will be priced highly and could become a status symbol for some, while being a functional necessity for others. An additional feature will be a paging system that will not only give an alarm to the subscriber that he is wanted, but will also display the caller's number.

For better performance of the telesystem, there is a proposal to limit a local call to 3 minutes and a trunk call to 9 minutes. Under this proposal, a call in excess of 3 minutes will be billed as a second call (double the current charge). The proposal is to make local telephone calls time bound, with each call being metered on a 3-minute basis. There is urgent need to introduce this scheme to lower the load factor on the system and also to inculcate a sense of precision among telephone users, but the additional costs again make telephone service more expensive than the average citizen can afford.

There is also a proposal to introduce a Business Network System designed to divert high traffic for the business subscriber from the normal network, and to provide facilities like voice, data, telex, facsimile, videotex, and electronic manual service to the subscriber (presently, these services are only available to private businesses).

There has been a proposal to establish an "overlay" telecommunication network for business, industry, and other priority areas. In this network, a subscriber would be connected by either optical fiber or radio telephone to a nodal exchange/switching center that would communicate nationwide through roof-top microwave satellite terminals. Industrial users in backward or remote areas can hook into this network by using earth stations. An international gateway for international communication will be provided, but the proposed network will cover four metropolitan and eight second-level industrial towns. The packet-switched data network (PSDN) would interface with the public-switched telephone network (PSTN), public-switched packet data network, public telex network, and computer database.

The business network will thus provide four facilities that will provide telex, message, and interactive data communications at speeds of 300–1,200 bits per second using satellite technology. It will provide the capability of high speed data transmission between computers as well as interactive access from telex, PSTN, and data terminals to such computers. It will also provide for electronic mail and would have access to the low speed business data network and could accommodate voice and data.

The introduction of such a network would provide internationally compatible telecommunication services and would provide the impetus for establishing modern national integrated communication systems. Not only will business networks boost trade and industry, but thousands of nonsubscribers would benefit by reducing the load on existing exchanges and providing reliable and efficient telephone services.

Video- and AudioCassettes

The video technology used today facilitates local communication delivered to people in languages and dialects in a meaningful context. Through narrowcasting of special interest programs, the government has made video messages more accessible to a wider range of people than ever before.

Video parlors are set up by people in residential and commercial places both in the urban and rural areas to watch feature films and other programs that might interest them. These are voluntary efforts for effective, inexpensive entertainment and leisure-time activity. This distribution outlet facilitates communication effects of Indian cinema and development programs on a comparatively larger population hitherto neglected because of limited resources and reach.

The video parlors act like mobile cinemas and are very effective as a communication tool. India is the largest producer of feature films but, in the past, only 10% of its population could watch these films because of the inaccessibility to the cinema houses in urban areas. Now, however, video parlors have made these films available to a larger percentage of the population.

The video technology is having a wide use and applicability as people use video for leisure-time entertainment at home. They like to watch movies in the privacy of their homes, at their own convenience, and inexpensively rather than going to the cinema. Those who cannot afford to have their own sets make good use of video parlors to entertain themselves. The broadcasters use video for special interest TV programs, sitcoms and TV films. Video is also being used for specialized educational purposes in medicine, engineering, agriculture, and so forth, and the people of India have received video and television with great interest and a positive attitude.

In the 1980s when video technology became a possible distribution medium for home consumption, the government had three major concerns—the social impact of video, video piracy, and low indigenous manufacture of the hardware. As an adjunct to the Asia Games, the government allowed a video boom to occur by reducing import fees and customs charges for videocassette recorders (VCRs). The reduced charges encouraged a greater adoption and diffusion of the VCRs, and encouraged the perspective that if technology is made available at low cost, the hardware will diffuse rapidly to a larger audience. This is an example of the event preceding policy operation, a common technology-driven argument for adopting a new distribution form.

Today the government is mainly concerned with the social impact of video technology such as the uncensored wide circulation of violent and sex-oriented programs shown in these video parlors. Questions surrounding the possible undesirable effects on the public's morals and morale are common. Therefore, the government is planning for a policy of regulating and censoring the programs in video parlors and video programs that are available in the video markets in India as well as licensing these video parlors.

Like many other nations, another concern is that of video piracy. At present, there is no regular system of taping videocassette programs in the country as well as payment of royalties for such taped programs. Most copies of Indian films have been pirated, severely affecting the Indian film industries by cutting attendance in cinema houses, and raising the question of copyright and royalty payments. These problems have prompted the government to pass legislation in 1986 making it compulsory for video shops selling program cassettes and the video parlors to pay royalties on video program cassettes.

Another concern is the low indigenous manufacture of hardware. At present, neither the public nor private sector is manufacturing blank video- or audiocassettes in the country. Most of them are being imported. But by its recent (1986) modification in industrial and communication policies, the government has licensed private sectors to manufacture audio- and videocassettes and audio and video recorders (although not video cameras) by transfer, import, and by making use of indigenous technology. This will help make the consumer's access to video technology comparatively inexpensive. The use of audiocassettes and cassette recorders have contributed to the development of communication and entertainment. They are now marketed inexpensively in India and have revolutionized the entertainment field like transistors did in the late 1960s and early 1970s. But they have to make better progress for educational development purposes.

The government has become increasingly concerned about the proliferation of video ads attached to videocassette distribution. All videocassette production emanates from private production centers, and advertising agencies are increasingly looking toward including ads on videocassettes for mass distribution. The government's concerns focus on the fee structure for advertising. If an ad is placed on television, the government receives some revenue from the advertiser, but when the advertiser goes to a private production house and has ads placed on a different distribution channel (the video-cassette), the government loses out on potential revenue.

The use of cassettes (video and audio) can facilitate both formal and nonformal education and have capitalized on the special distribution needs of special audiences. Although the government has encouraged use of cassettes for formal education in schools and universities both for internal purposes and to telecast to other institutions; open university centers use them in a nonbroadcast mode. All formal education programs are produced and financed by the University Grants Commission. With special production centers throughout India, the production quality of these houses is very good. A special approach to using these pre-produced, telecast materials incorporates how they are coordinated in the overall educational curriculum. Recent research indicates that many students find the language difficult to comprehend, and if the school does not schedule discussion sections with a teacher present (the typical broadcast day of Indian national television is from 6 p.m. to 11 p.m.), the rest of the programming day is available for educational TV, but not all hours are compatible with the hours of certain educational institutions. Therefore, if the school does not make an effort to integrate the educational material into the curriculum, the students find the material either too difficult to understand or to assimilate.

Nonformal education has focused on social education (traffic instructions, road safety, railway protocol and information, and airport guides), and for development education (family planning programs, prevention of disease, environmental concerns, and home safety). Public displays have been established at busy intersections, driver training schools, and driver traffic parks for children, and TV monitors on street corners instruct pedestrians on negotiating their safety. Audiocassettes in specially staffed kiosks give instructions in the predominant languages in each area.

Hospitals have used cassette materials for preventative medicine, and have encouraged use of these materials for outside patients, in lobbies, for health professionals, and so on. Industries have used them extensively for training tapes; agricultural extension workers have used them for continuing education and demonstrations, and banking institutions have used them for internal and outreach purposes. In-house and corporate video has also enhanced product identification and to facilitate realty transactions, travel plans, and other such uses.

Another issue that concerns both the government and the masses is the division of what gets carried through traditional television versus the cassette-distribution medium. For example, railway safety has been packaged for mass consumption by television through a prosocial approach toward educating the railway passenger on safety. When more messages can be distributed via television or videocassette to a largely illiterate public, there is less demand for personal attention at the information counter.

An interesting trend in the use of videocassettes in religious temples has involved taped ceremonies shown particularly at festival times. This re-addresses the role of the priest, but the videocassettes have become very popular for some people at these special times. Within India and abroad, the use of videocassettes to spread the messages of religious leaders and the opportunity to view participants engaging in religious discourse, has become popular through the efforts of ashrams to spread their messages. The many pilgrimage places throughout India have begun to use video- and audiocas-settes to simultaneously translate religious observances for worshipers of different language groups. Therefore, a pilgrim from the south may travel to one of the holy centers in the north, yet have his or her own language accompany the rituals throughout the observance.

Like the videotaped religious ceremonies, audiocassettes are now available to the people with religious music, segments of ceremonies, and special events. This interesting mixture of technology and tradition suggests an effective use of technology within a social context.

Cassettes (both video and audio) have limited use due to distribution exigencies, and only a few agencies have produced their own cassette prod-ucts within an indigenous context. For example, agriculture, family planning institutes, specialized medical institutes and health concerns have produced realistic cassettes with Indian actors, dealing with Indian issues. Many of the other users of these software forms use materials produced outside of the country, and thus, present images that are not compatible with the Indian situations.

Cassettes have been used for tourism purposes such as explanations of historical and cultural issues. These are particularly used on sight at historical monuments, for historical figures, and popular tourist spots.

Some institutions, such as the Indian public and specialized libraries (including the National Library) have not seized the opportunity to make audio–video facilities available to users. Schools for the handicapped have made greater use of cassette materials (particularly audiocassettes for the blind).

Computer Technologies

Throughout the 1980s the government and business organizations attempted to use computers on a large scale. In the 1960s, India wanted to computerize functions of banking, insurance, the airlines, telephones, hotel reservations, libraries, and voting in national elections, but at that time there was neither indigenous hardware or software to back it up. The country planned to import both, but the attempt was not successful because many people feared that the use of computers would usurp their jobs. At that time, no amount of persuasion could convince and make those people accept the fact that computerization would create more jobs in the particular fields, but that they would mean less time spent on traditional performances.

At that point the government could not initiate computerization against the majority of people's wishes, but a move toward these ends began to create an awareness among the people. A few large industrial houses did import computers and computerized their functions on a small scale, particularly in the area of data analysis. The government also continued to use computerization for its national planning forecasts and planning procedures for its National Development plans. Some of the physical sciences and social science institutes used computerization for data analysis purposes only, and few basic computer courses were taught in the various institutes of technology in the country.

The government approached computerization by attempting to foster a computer literacy in the country, and by developing a plan to produce computers indigenously. It also liberalized its policy for the import of computers, transfer of technology for computer hardware and software production, and allowed the indigenous production of computers on a large scale. Not long ago, the plans started to use computers in major government networks. The net result was that between 1983 and 1987, the functioning of major networks and areas of airlines, banking, insurance, transportation, defense, telecommunications, scientific and technological applications, space travel, government police, mass communication, hospitals, hotel reservations, and big business are computerized areas. Computer science and engineering courses are being offered in technology institutes and universities. The private organizations are also offering short-term computer courses for software and data processing.

At present, the indigenous production of computers is limited to large computers and micro and mini computers, but this has helped in a big way. It is estimated that 50,000 families possess home computers and many more use them in offices. The manufacture of computers may not be a losing proposition if there are "economies of scale," but domestic consumption being low, exports have to be encouraged. An electronic infrastructure is needed, and the significant factors for the diffusion of computers are technical, financial, and marketing considerations.

Millions of dollars are being invested on developing a new computer culture in India. This includes the indigenous resources, assistance from developed countries and various UN agencies that are providing technical expertise, hardware, and planners. The UNDP project specifically aims at creating a cultural revolution in Indian Industries on the use of microprocessor technology.

Five regional sectors—Bangalore, Jabalpur, New Delhi, Pune, and Ranchi—have been set up in the country for special sectors such as agriculture, communications, steel manufacturing, and mines; electronics and industrial control. Projects on microprocessor use have started in utility sectors such as environment control, transport, and aeronautics. Two key projects, both microprocessor-based computer-aided learning systems are planned at Bangalore.

A computer-controlled system is being developed for satellite-based communication network software. Packages are being developed for graphic terminals, and microcomputer-based data acquisition systems. Microprocessor-based agriculture equipment is being developed to complete the green revolution, and the UN is assisting the development of basic health-care and electromedical equipment for more than 30,000 primary health centers throughout the country.

Another major UN-assisted project is setting up knowledge-based and fifth-generation computer systems involving artificial intelligence. India has also been negotiating with both the United States and the Soviet Union for a super computer to be used for defense purposes. A national software center is being set up in Bhuboneshwar in the Orissa state. The sites planned for two super computers are Hyderabad and Pune, with a central computer site in New Delhi.

The current concern of developing countries including India is that computers may be taken to rural areas and made more meaningful with applications aimed at improving the lot of people in rural areas by microlevel planning for food and agriculture, education, health, communication, industries, banking, and the environment. Four major computerization projects include plans for schools, super computers, rail cargo movement, and the computerization of library and information services.

Computer Policy. A new computer policy was developed in November 1986 after reviewing the existing situation, and by discussions with computer manufacturers, experts, and economists. The government liberalized computer policies to make computers more available, to promote manufacturing within the country at comparable international prices, based on the latest technology, and to promote their application on a variety of resource-saving uses. The major components of the policy include the following:

1. no restriction on industrial capacity for manufacture of micro and mini computer systems;
2. reducing costs of inputs that are required for computers manufactured;
3. simplified procedures to enable users to obtain computers from indigenous or overseas sources;
4. micro and mini computers can be manufactured by an Indian company with 40% equity whether in private or public sectors. Manufac-

ture of mainframe and super mini computers were reserved for the public sector (ECIL) up to 1988. Since then, there has been an indigenization and ECIL will provide a horizontal transfer of knowledge in addition to import of transfer technology in this direction;

5. the government will also reduce duty on computer peripherals, such as disk drives, disks and printers, and so forth; and

6. duties on source codes for software makers to obtain source codes from their collaborators rather than object codes.

Computer Plans for Schools. The computer literacy and studies in school project (CLASS) was initiated in 1984. This project has been guided by specialists from the United Kingdom, which also has an aggressive program in place to teach computer skills in the schools, thereby reducing the knowledge gap and reticence of students toward computers and technology. The real aim has been to create a human power-base upon which a technologically capable work force could be built. The government sought to spread computer culture by training teachers from school and in turn to demystify technology for the students.

Such schools are represented in all geographical areas, particularly those whose student population comes largely from lower socioeconomic levels. Interestingly, the government has been aware of the need not to make computers the resources of the elites alone, but although there is tremendous interest in the program, a lack of infrastructure facilities has created a delay in developing computer curricula and advanced-level computer training in the schools.

The government hopes to extend the CLASS project to 250,000 schools by 1990. Initially, the United Kingdom donated computers to India when efforts to produce them within the country floundered because of low demand. Another problem occurred on the software front, as the CLASS computers could not keep pace with imported systems.

Experts feel inexpensive and economical home computers should replace the outdated and complicated CLASS computers. If and when home computers are available, the program would take a quantum leap and achieve the desired goals.

Super Computers. Although India is planning to manufacture its own super computer with indigenous as well as imported components, it approaches the problem of high-speed, high-volume computer traffic by cooperating with other countries. The United States provided the super computer cray-xmp with a 600 megaflop capacity that will be used for complicated aeronautical designs, defense purposes, and meteorological forecasts. India has also used the Cyber-205, developed in the United States, and an S-1000 super computer from Japan. This latter computer has 50-100 megaflops. Four units have been installed in the National Informatic system being built to process data from various government departments from district to national levels. Cooperation with the Soviet Union resulted in use of the ELBROS super computer, with 100 megaflop power.

Rail Cargo Computer Project. Computerization of a railway movement project is being aided by World Bank and under contract to Canadian railways. This computerization would keep a watch on the movement of each and every car with the railways and will provide continually updated data on working out the optimum use of these cars. At present in manual operations, railways face such situations as unused cars, while no cars are available for even essential use and unscrupulous traders in collusion with railway use cars to manipulate prices of goods. The computerization is expected to provide dramatic improvement in the railroad's productivity in freight movement and increase in revenue.

Computerization of the Library. There is slow progress in the computerization of library and information services in India because computer specialists have not realized the demand for such applications and therefore have not taken an interest in the development of the system for this subject field. Also, adequate training is not available for library documentation professionals in using computers for these services. Some of the larger library and information centers such as INSDOC and DESIDOC tried to recruit computer specialists but could not attract them for the library-based computerization activities. There is a need for computerization of library/information services as well as use of heuristic systems (ES).

Satellite Communication

Satellites are already supplying limited telephone, television, and radio services in addition to meteorological data and other forms of service throughout India on 12 C-band frequencies. Two extra powerful S-band channels are giving direct telecast facilities from satellites to small home antennae in rural areas.

INSAT IB is a unique joint venture of the Department of Space (DOS), Posts and Telegraphs (Ministry of Communication), Meteorological Department (Ministry of Tourism and Civil Aviation), Doordarshan (the television service), and All India Radio (Ministry of Information and Broadcasting). Although the DOS has the responsibility of hardware establishment, the operation and maintenance of the space segment, other concerned departments have been entrusted with preparation of their respective ground segments. For example, Doordarshan (the television production facility) plans and produces television software for the rural communities, as well as for other target groups.

INSAT 1B has the capabilities for nation-wide coverage by direct telecast to augment low-cost community receiver sets, television, and radio program distribution and networking, disaster warning and relay of hydrological/ meteorological/oceanographic data from unattended land and ocean-based data transmission platforms.

Through INSAT 1B, in addition to nation-wide television coverage, it has become possible to provide national networking of all the existing transmitters in order to facilitate program exchange between different Doordarshan Kendras. Thus, INSAT television has two distinct features: direct telecast, and nation-wide networking using existing terrestrial transmitters.

With this arrangement, important events are being covered and distributed live to all parts of the country. The major advantage of this system, however, is to provide television service to the remote rural and backward areas of the country where developmental efforts require mass media support.

Under INSAT, specific clusters in six states: Andhra Pradesh, Bihar, Guijarat, Maharashtra, Orissa, and Uttar Pradesh have been identified for coverage. Criteria for targeting these areas was made based on the underdevelopment of the areas, availability of suitable physical and developmental infrastructures, and utilization of existing television program production facilities. The selection of these clusters has been made in such a way that the widest possible range of experience from the projects in different cultural and linguistic settings would be obtained for future expansion in other parts of the country. In the sixth 5-year plan, 2,000 VHF sets will be installed in five selected states for community viewing in rural areas.

The instructional objectives of INSAT television cover the areas of agricultural productivity, health, hygiene, family welfare, formal and nonformal education, national integration, and so on. According to the organizer of the project, Yash Pal (1984) in pursuance of the objectives, the thrust of the area specific programs is to:

- provide development instructions in support of the extension methodologies in the field of agricultural productivity;

- stimulate participation and involvement in extension activities that will directly benefit the rural people, particularly the weaker and the underprivileged sections;

- provide instructions for better public health and hygiene living, including messages in family welfare;

- move away from a curriculum oriented approach, emphasizing direct teaching and aim at improving the quality of education in classrooms as well as through teacher-training programs;

- emphasize science education in order to promote a scientific temper;
- help promote social justice; and
- stimulate public interest in news and current affairs, games, sports, and other important events.

Because in the initial stages programs will be uplinked from Delhi, capsuled programs will have to be sent to Delhi well in advance from the program production centers established at different clusters. Satellites could also facilitate other forms of communication, such as the transmission by facsimile of newspapers and magazines for various regions. Eighty-thousand copies of a newspaper (e.g., going from India to West Asia) will cost $6,000 per day in airfreight. The airfreight bill for a week will pay for facsimile equipment to last a decade.

Other computerized equipment has also begun to make a big impact in India. Organizations unwilling to invest from $1,000 to $10,000 per editorial staff members employed will find themselves working without the right tools in a highly competitive world.

The major concerns for satellite use include: (a) optimum utilization of satellite capacity, and (b) how much of the broadcast mode will be utilized for development programs particularly localized programs. This is significant because of regional subcultural and language diversity. This presents not technological challenges per se, but also cultural challenges. The model that will be useful will be development programs integrating broadcast and telematics.

Social Technology: Telecommunication

There is an implicit assumption that telecommunication investments will help integrate and modernize the nation and society, and that they will improve education and training. More rapid dissemination of modernizing ideas would enhance the ability of the telecommunication system to reach more people, and likewise, more people will think favorably of an enhanced communication system. The current migration toward already overpopulated cities could change, and governmental planning could find a firmer and safer footing. What is important to keep in mind, however, is that unless the social technologies are compatible with the media technologies, few projections can be made about utility and effectiveness.

The expectations are that there will be "growth" through telecommunication services as they replace transport and energy costs in a cheap and efficient way. They will enhance industrial coordination and planning through better insight in supplies, prices, and market forces, and could develop the tourism industry by making possible efficient booking, transportation, and accommodations. In rural areas, it could stimulate agriculture through more insight of the individual farmer in the market, with a knowledge of price and demand, and it will help distribute development aid more equitably.

The telephone subscriber in India has traditionally experienced problems on both the micro and macro levels. Public complaints range from inefficient directory inquiries to operational problems of handling public complaints by departments. The public has problems such as billing and payment of bills, wrong numbers, and cross connections due to old and outdated exchanges and little air conditioning, which prevents the equipment from functioning properly. Low use of STD (domestic direct dialing) facilities due to corrupt practices of charging bills for calls that have not been made are also problems experienced in the past, and the responsiveness of the telephone company has been regarded with scorn by the people.

The growth of urbanization is also putting more pressure on effective communication in public places. Hospitals, busstops, railway stations, and many other public places require phones even if a home receiver is not absolutely necessary.

With growing urbanization, this is an inevitable necessity and helps to ease the pressure on transport by reducing physical movement. The old idea that the telephone is a luxury for the rich has been outgrown, but the realities have still worked to constrain the average citizen from getting a telephone connection due to high cost. For example, for a home consumer, the cost (as of 1989) for the connection is 7,000 rupees (approximately $500 U.S.) to register for that connection. Once registered, it may take 5 to 7 years before the telephone is installed. To access a connection within a month, the cost is approximately 3,000 rupees. The installation charges, bi-monthly rental charges are 300 rupees, and each call is at minimum 2 rupees. The capability to connect more telephones exists, but the costs have not been reduced so that the average citizen can afford the service. Telephony is no longer a luxury, but is still priced as though it were. The government needs to address these issues, bring costs down, increase availability, and offer incentives to the masses to use the system.

Cultural Challenges

As previously stated, in India the government perspective is that the use of science and technology should be to accelerate the pace of development by informing, educating, and motivating people, and that these elements should create an efficient communication network for a larger number of people.

The masses perspective is that communications technologies should be easily available as well as accessible, cost effective, efficient, and should give meaningful performance; therefore, it should provide a better quality of life.

Both the government and masses perspectives are related by the cultural challenges each of these perspectives provide. For example, the government's cultural challenges have to do with providing technologies for pro-social purposes within the multiculturally diverse population. The cultural challenges for the people have to do with their abilities to assimilate material within their own social systems. These two positions come together in the way both address (a) the use of existing technologies for disseminating information and prosocial messages to diverse regional subcultures, and (b) the implementation of homogeneity within the limited economic and technological resources for a concept of "unity culture" and national identity.

Indian culture is a pluralistic culture with a set of subcultures comprised of regional cultures. The cultural resources of subcultures are diverse, and when different participants from various regional subcultures interact, they put their cultural resources at risk. The result could be amalgamation, integration, adoption, negotiation, or certain cultural sacrifices.

The challenges provided by information techologies facilitate the speed with which different subcultures interact, but the economic imperatives caused by increased technology bring even more challenges to the fore. If privatization of large infrastructurally related technologies and the challenge for use of modern technological and management styles and behaviors threatens traditional cultures, but if they can be integrated in a nonthreatening manner, the traditional cultures need not be at great risk. What must be strived for is a development of social competence to deal with technological changes and value orientations.

THE INFORMATION TECHNOLOGY MODEL IN INDIA

The information technology model in India has been developed for social transformation in the country to give information power to people by diffusing information at a grassroots level (for more details on mobilizing grassroots movements, see Narula 1990). The whole model is based on three social principles of connectivity, social accessibility to the system, and reliability of the system (see Fig. 4.1).

The model has three major foci: (a) a national focus to develop a technology model based on advanced technology; (b) the focus to apply, link, and accept technology in people's lifestyles and social systems; and (c) the focus on the information bureaucracy which initiates a technology according to value options and technology options. When these two options do not match, the outcome may be an application of low technology rather than the

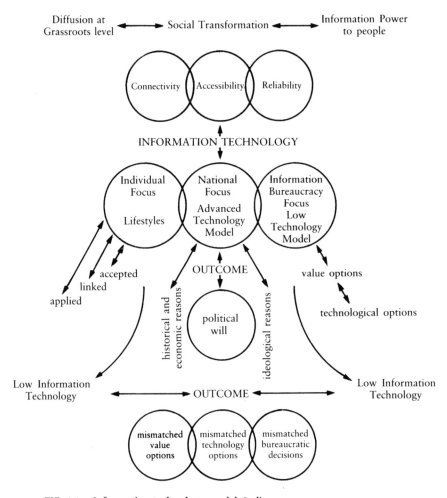

FIG. 4.1.   Information technology model: India.

advanced technology model as accepted by national focus, but the matching IT culture may not develop because of mismatched values and options. For example, the speed of a facsimile message may be lost if the person is lethargic in picking up the message. Efficiency of banking may be lost if the facility for all India computer networks linking various banks for clearing of local or outstation cheques is not used. Therefore, instead of instantaneous transfer of money the customer may have to wait for 3 to 15 days.

The mismatching technology option and the bureaucratic decisions may also result in the adoption of low technology though national focus may be

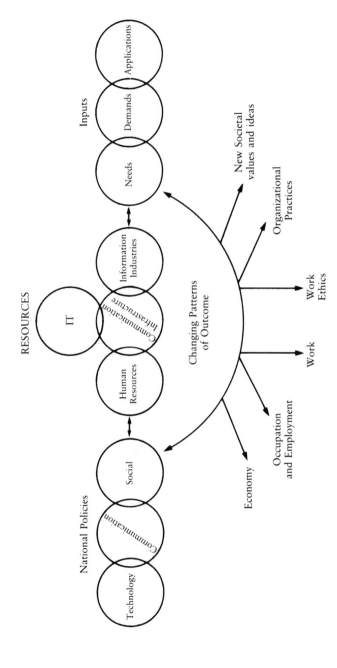

FIG. 4.2. Information society model: India.

73

for high technology. The India model is a pro-social model different from the western model that emphasizes patterns of economy and work.

The Information Society Model

The development of an information technology (IT) culture depends on human resources, communication infrastructure, and information technology industries. How IT culture in a society develops depends on two factors. First, the national policies for technological, communication, and social policies, and second, the needs and demands for an applications of information technology (see Fig. 4.2).

When resources, national policies, needs, and demands for an applications of information technology interact with each other the outcome may be many, such as changing patterns of the economy, occupation and employment, patterns of work, work ethics and organizational practices, and the infiltration of new values and ideas in society.

SUMMARY

The information technology model is undergoing development phases in which more and more is being expanded updated, from the perspective of hardware technology, social technology, the cultural context, and its challenges. The upcoming Indian information society and information models are indications that a Third World nation can be optimistic, revitalized, and can include a more people-oriented communication system.

Like some of the other Asian nations, India has taken the burden of development and has made choices that will inevitably effect the lives of all of her people. Many of the lessons have not come easily or painlessly to India, but the strong integration of development policies and plans with an acknowledgment of how people interect within their traditional cultures, indicates that a unique model of development may already be underway.

India's Border Nations, ASEAN, and Pacific Communities: Case Studies

It must be emphasized though, that few, if any, information systems are qualified as the indigenous media to preserve a people's culture and traditions. It will be up to the policy makers to find the path by which traditional media can best serve the people and strengthen their heritage in the forthcoming technological age.
—Meheroo Jussawalla and Debra Lynn Hughs (1984)

Nations sharing India's borders and those from Southeast Asia and the Pacific Rim have widely divergent experiences with development and information technology. What they share, however, is a strong sense of tradition that often guides both governments and the social interactions of the masses. The countries in these regions are varied in size, population, and economic potential; with high capacity investment countries with advanced technology infrastructures like Japan and Australia, and countries like India and China, where the size of the country and human resources lend themselves to indigenous production of technology. Still, there are other countries that are smaller and have human resources and industrial policies that create markets for industrialized countries.

The nations that share India's borders and those of the ASEAN and Pacific regions represent widely discrepant levels of development for several reasons. Some of the reasons have to do with traditional geographic and economic problems; many others have to do with how some of those nations have entered the information society as producers of software goods to the exclusion of developing or integrating hardware for their own purpose.

Rapid changes in policy matters and organizational structures are taking place within the ASEAN telecommunications industries. Changes in regulatory and economic environments are introducing new concepts of regulation, institutional structures, pricing policies, and financial structures of the information economy. Although the overall picture of these nations may appear to be reassuring, a closer look is less encouraging.

In this chapter we explore many of these nations. We do not claim that this chapter is inclusive of all nations from each region because some that would fit into this category are highly industrialized, like Japan, or are significantly more "developed" like Hong Kong and Taiwan. Our purpose for including those nations we do describe is to continue our theme of national development plans that focus on media and social technologies. Therefore, we have chosen representative nations from the region that offer unique perspectives to developing nations and the information society.

What becomes apparent in the country descriptions that follow is the wide imbalance of technologies and services among these nations. "The Asia Pacific region comprising 55 percent of the world's population has only 103 million of the world's 600 million telephones. Many of the nations in the region have a telephone density that is less than 1 percent" (Thongma, 1988, p. 22; see Table 5.1, below).

Like India, many of these nations have enormous rural populations that complicate matters for development. Other characteristics that enter into the discussions include long-standing traditions and customs that influence the diffusion of technologies and new ideas, and in some parts, illiteracy, although reading is highly prized by some of these nations and the traditions of print are long and impressive (see Table 5.2).

One common characteristic of the nations included in this chapter is that each has a population growing at a rate of between .9% and 2.3% per year.

TABLE 5.1
Telephones Per 1,000 Inhabitants (Figures Reported for 1985,
Unless Otherwise Indicated)

Singapore	30.96	
Brunei Darusallem	9.27	
Malaysia	6.11	
Thailand	1.21	
Philippines	0.88	
China	0.58	
Pakistan	0.48	
Sri Lanka	0.47	(1986)
Indonesia	0.31	(1982)
Burma	0.12	(1983)
Nepal	0.12	
Bangladesh	n/a	
Vietnam	n/a	

TABLE 5.2
Comparative Percentage of Illiteracy in Population

Country	Year of report and percentage of illiteracy		1985 report
Nepal	1972	79.3	74.4
Indonesia	1980	32.7	25.9
Bhutan	—		—
Bangladesh	1981	70.8	66.9
Burma	—		—
Cambodia	—		—
Sri Lanka	1981	13.2	12.9
Laos	—		16.1
Malaysia	1980	42.0	26.6
Pakistan	1981	73.8	70.4
Thailand	1980	12.0	70.4
Vietnam	1979	16.00	—

Sources: UNESCO (1987a, 1987b for 1985 figures).

(*Far East and Australasia*, 1987) creating development stress in housing, education, health care, nutrition and women's pre- and postnatal needs. The number of children of educatable age will continue to create an imbalance in agricultural production, growth of cities, and disbursement of resources throughout various regions.

In many cases, migration has played a significant role in cross-cultural ideas and technological innovation. Migrants who have gone to other countries or migrated from one region to another in their own countries, have upset traditional social structures.

Another important factor to keep in mind is the proximity of many of these nations to others, creating population drifts and cultural exchanges along historic, religious, cultural, and linguistic lines. The nations represented in this chapter all represent meeting grounds of cultural forces that, when faced with change, handle the challenges in different ways. For the most part, change (primarily through and by technological means) is effecting urban dwellers, who make up the smallest percentage of each nation. Yet, the development presented often is affected by political forces from within the country, and often, from without, such as the targeting of Thailand and Singapore as havens for multinational corporation activity.

Their geographic location also facilitates the interaction between Japan and Australia, and other neighbors. Both of these industrial giants offer technical assistance to surrounding countries, and governments in the region have adopted policies to encourage foreign manufacturing.

As indicated in the introduction to this chapter many of these nations are progressing at widely divergent rates. Some nations like Indonesia, are progressing rather rapidly due to successful monetary and fiscal policy changes, despite its recent past frought with a slump in oil and the effects of a largely yen-dominated foreign debt (Davey, 1988). Some other nations, like Burma, Laos, and Vietnam have lacked cohesive development plans and are therefore only beginning to look at internal issues for change in telecommunications. Yet, some other nations (like Singapore) are finding themselves swept up in an information society at one level of production for export, which is introducing problems on a wide range of levels of change. Some of the countries, such as Bhutan, Timor, Nepal, the Cook Islands, Kirabati, Nauru, Ninue, Norfolk Islands, Papua-New Guinea, the Solomon Islands, Tonga, and Vanuatu still do not have their own television services (Abundo, 1987; UNESCO, 1986).

Telecommunication Growth

In his presentation to the eighth annual Pacific Telecommunications Conference in Sendai Japan, Graham J. Davey (1988), the ITU Area Representative for Southeast Asia stated that there is still a need for:

1. further reduction in equipment power consumption,
2. better corrosion protection,
3. reduced air conditioning demand,
4. more reliable power supply systems, and
5. continuing improvement of equipment in general.

Furthermore, he advocated that fiber optics should be replacing co-axial cable, and that the newly developing countries are in the position of introducing Integrated Services Digital Network (ISDN) before that becomes state-of-the-art for many industrialized countries.

Regional Cooperation

The Asian Telecommunications Network (ATN) was established in the late 1960s to act as a professional resource within the region. One of its activities was to establish the Asia Pacific Telecommunity (APT) to "realize a balanced development of inter-and intra-regional networks" (Thongma, 1988, p. 22) to coordinate development efforts in the South Pacific, the ASEAN subre-gion, and the South Asian (SAARC) regions. To assist in this goal, the APT has undertaken three programs:

1. Quality of service project; to carry out on-site surveys and assist in developing action plans, usually through visits with teams of experts.

2. Development of Rural Networks Project; to do feasibility studies for greater telecommunications coverage.

3. Technological advance and new services; to concentrate on appropriate technologies for regions with appropriate costs for entire populations. The primary emphasis in this area has been on the development of digital technologies.

Many communication training and research centers have been developed throughout the region, and there is much in the way of broadcast and news reciprocity. One of the most notable centers for training is the Asia Pacific Institute of Broadcasting Development (AIBD).

Likewise, endeavors have been made to create a computer network that connects six members of the ASEAN region with Australia. The network, named AuseaNet, provides an alternative to the usual commercial international networks, and is based on a long distance interpersonal network developed by NETWORK Lab of Indonesia. The new network will enhance the exchange of information on microelectronic technology between the Philippines, Brunei, Indonesia, Malaysia, Singapore, and Thailand. AuseaNet will also help users strengthen their capabilities in the fabrication and applications of microelectronics, and will provide user friendly interfaces to transfer files, electronic mail and provide bulletin board services (*Asia Computer Weekly*, 1989).

Plans are already under way for indigenously produced satellites to facilitate data transfer among nations of the regions. The Pakistani Satellite Badr-A is to be launched in 1990, and a Korean satellite is scheduled for launch during 1997.

THE GOVERNMENT PERSPECTIVES

In many of the countries discussed here, colonial domination by Great Britain or France has left legacies that have influenced the structures of government. Some of the nations have chosen to follow in the footsteps of their former colonizers, others have entered into a period of changing government due to pressures from the masses or specific interest groups. Because of their strategic locations, many of the countries discussed in this chapter have been battlegrounds (literally or figuratively) for military domination by industrialized nations. Likewise, their value as political alliances have influenced domestic as well as international activity and plans for operation within the information society.

In some countries of the region, government policies adhere to Islamic practices. The tenets of Islam maintain that all laws should be those that further Islamic principles and practices. Therefore, in many of the Moslem countries policies that restrict the use of content that may be pornographic may be in place. What constitutes pornography is another issue. For example, anything that is sexually explicit may be considered pornography, but so may women's bodies in scantily clad clothing. Material that spreads thoughts against Islam is also considered in this category, and therefore media that concentrates on figure studies of powerful leaders who oppose Islamic nations or their leaders may be included.

Policies toward imports and technological transfer are also a major issue for governments. In Pakistan, a liberal import policy to encourage micro computers in business was seen as a way of encouraging small business development, but it had the added dimension of increasing the number of television sets, videocassette recorders, and micro computers used by other members of society who could afford them, and fostered an environment that brought in many illegal pieces of software.

THE MASSES PERSPECTIVES

In societies rich in tradition, the issue of change is a very complex one. Wang and Dissanayake (1984) have collected a number of essays that speak about specific nations, problems, and methods of retaining traditional societies despite the intrusion of communication technologies. Many of these societies are founded on traditions of news from other parts of the world coming from traders, religious persons, or balladeers. The importance of these traditional channels of information cannot be overlooked; the importance of art as communication is deeply ingrained in many of the cultures. For most of these regions then, tradition should be considered as a component of development. The masses' need for some consistency and a veneration of traditional practices is highly valued.

In many of the cultures discussed in this chapter, the value of education and a desire for literacy already exists; and therefore adaptation to other media that is print based is less of a challenge than in a society where leapfrogging from an oral culture to an electronic one is occurring.

Within these regions telephones and televisions are limited (see Tables 5.1 and 5.3), sometimes because of a lack of electricity, but the preponderance of VCRs is surprisingly high. Most of the available technology is in urban areas, and therefore tends to benefit few of the individuals who make up society.

The masses in these regions have a wide variety of basic needs to consider. The life expectancy of a person in Laos is only 30 to 35 years. To address problems of disease, and the concerns of other basic needs, technologies have been used in many of these regions to aid in education.

TABLE 5.3
Radio Versus TV Receivers, 1975–1985

Country	Radio Receivers (per thousand)		TV Receivers (per thousand)	
	1975	1985	1975	1985
Bangladesh	—	40	0.3	3
Bhutan		14	—	0.5
Burma	—	81	—	—
Indonesia	37	117	2.2	39
Malaysia	115	424	36	101
Nepal	9	30	—	1.2
Pakistan	54	90	5.1	13
Sri Lanka	51	—	—	28
Thailand	126	175	—	97
Vietnam	—	100	—	33

Source: UNESCO (1987b).

INDIA'S BORDER NATIONS

Pakistan

Even predating the independence on August 14, 1947, regional differences with India had created poor relations between the predominantly Moslem area that became Pakistan, and India. Today, 97% of the population in the region known as Pakistan are Moslems, and only 3% represent Christians, Hindus, and Farsis (Pakistan facts and figures, 1987, p. 6). Violence has been experienced at times between different sects of Moslems, complicating the structures of society, and often expected or traditional behaviors may be different in those sects. For example, the most economically successful are the non-Sunni, who represent the minority of Moslems, and this sometimes exaccerbates problems among the largest, Sunni group.

The presence of the Moslem faith dictates how and why some social arrangements exist as they do (more is discussed in the chapter on Arab nations), but the geographic region of Pakistan acts as a bridge between the Middle East and South-East Asia, further exaccerbating tensions among neighbors and complicating domestic matters.

Within Pakistan, however, there are strata of society that are perceived to have more status than others. Landlords are pivotal figures in rural relations, as are farmers and priests. Following these people in the social hierarchy are the craftsmen, although there are some crafts, such as cobblers, who join the ranks of sweepers, garbage collectors, and latrine cleaners in the lowest echelon. There is a very small elite and middle class compared to the number of peasants and urban poor, but it is the family that is the basis for social relations.

Pakistan shares her borders with some distinctly different cultures such as China, Afghanistan, Iran, and India, but as is typical, border communities often set up their own dynamics for an even more complex cultural challenge. Six languages are present in Pakistan—Urdu, the national language, Punjabi, Sindhi, Pushto, Baliechi, and Brahvi.

Pakistan was created with an ideological philosophy articulated by Jinnah:

> The establishment of Pakistan, for which we have been striving for the last 10 years, is today, by the grace of God, an established fact. The idea was that we should have a state in which we could develop according to our own genius and culture and where principles of Islamic social justice could find freeplay. (Marker, 1987, p. 4)

This philosophy still predominates in government as President Zia pushes for more fundamentalism and also strives to get development money from the nearby oil-rich Middle East and North Africa (MENA) countries. As a result, many Pakistanis migrate to Arab nations to work, at least for some time. When they return home they often bring other ideas with them that may not be compatible with Pakistan's official government policies.

For example, the VCR has become a status symbol among migrants returning to Pakistan after working elsewhere. Along with hardware brought in to the country, the market for illicit videocassettes has thrived. Since 1956 Indian movies have been banned in Pakistan, but pirated copies have turned up just after a few days of release in one of India's many movie houses (Jabbar, 1983). Other bans on program content from other countries have also been violated, such as the pirated duplication of the movie *Gandhi*, which was considered to have slighted the founder of Pakistan.

Pakistan is still largely a feudal society with low literacy (see Table 5.2) and largely dependent on agriculture. No official development plans existed prior to 1978, but since that time a series of 5-year plans have been implemented. Part of the sixth development plan (1983–1988) included several features of telecommunication growth (Handbook of National Development Plans, 1988).

Part of the cultural challenges faced by Pakistan include the increasing move toward the cities from rural areas, and the rapid growth in the population. The sixth 5-year plan's goal of universal primary school education to be available for males, and to increase attendance of females from 33% to 45% (Nyrop, 1984) includes the use of radio distributed by satellite as an educational tool. Almost 50% of the radio broadcasts are dedicated to educational purposes (Akhtar, 1985) to further Islamic teachings.

In the past, most of the radio and television services (through PTV-Pakistan Television) have been focused on urban areas, but the sixth 5-year plan includes extending reach to four other regions and the establishment of a second channel for educational television. Pakistan uses microwave and satellite links to cover the rural regions, and to connect with many international carriers.

In 1986 the Department of Telegraph and Telephone introduced an electronic mail service and FAX service from Karachi to other foreign countries. The transmission service began with the Gulf countries, and was then linked among other cities in Pakistan and other countries (Pakistan will accelerate ... 1986, p. 4).

At a National Computer Conference in April 1986, Federal Minister of Science and Technology, Hamid Nasir Chattha, emphasized the importance of accelerating computer development in Pakistan, and announced plans to provide one microcomputer in every college and university over a 2-year period with the eventual goal of putting them in high schools as well (Pakistan will accelerate ... 1986, p. 4).

Pakistan's first domestic satellite was launched in 1988 to collect data in hydrology and mineral resources, and to assist in agriculture development. A proposal for launching an RS 400 million communications satellite has been submitted to the Cabinet for approval.

One major problem for development in Pakistan is the lack of sources of electricity. To study this problem, the government has established a Council for Scientific and Industrial Research and an Atomic Energy Commission (UNESCO, 1970).

Bangladesh

The young nation that emerged from the 1971 liberation war between India and Pakistan has endeavored to use the mass media to educate men and women about civic rights. Some of the cultural challenges include a large rural population (95%), a literacy rate of approximately 20%, and little availability of electricity. By 1987, almost half (45.7%) of the population was under the age of 14 (Kurian, 1987).

Most of the remaining telecommunications systems were originally instituted by the British to facilitate their rule, and today's society is heavily dominated by the various religious groups. The Moslems dominate society in number (85%–90%), followed by Hindus and a small number of Buddhists and Christians (Nyrop, Benderly, Conn, Cover, & Eglin).

Bangladesh has one of the lowest telephone densities in the world. Radio is a state activity, but has a limited audience. Television began in 1964 as a small government-supported commercial venture, and was nationalized by the new government in 1971, although it reaches a very small portion of society (approximately 15%). There is one satellite ground station to aid in domestic transfer of communications.

Many of the same development problems found in Pakistan are present in Bangladesh where, according to Ganley and Ganley (1987):

> Illegal VCRs of Indian movies which are not allowed in Bangladesh, and uncensored western films, some of which may be pornographic by even western standards, are freely available and widely watched in Bangladesh. Many video clubs for rentals and illegal video parlors exist and private owernship of VCRs is very widespread among families that can afford them. (p. 135)

Nepal

When H. M. King Birendra Bir Bikram Shah was coronated in 1975, he decreed that Nepal would be a land of peace. Since that time he has also decreed that no military groups would be allowed to be housed on Nepalese soil. Although these moves may be considered either progressive or problematic, the problems of Nepal are far more basic. Part of the fifth 5-year plan (1975–1980) included goals to meet minimum needs of people such as food and fuel (firewood); drinking water; basic health care; and the development of primary, vocational, and adult education.

Past plans have laid down basic infrastructure goals needed for development, but they have not been very effective, and have been hampered by a large increase in population. Goals in the sixth plan (1980–1985) have included the development of hydroelectric power, as the nation experiences increases in demand at a rate of approximately 2.8% per year, and estimated to continue at that rate until 1990 (Handbook of National Development Plans, 1988, Vol. II, pp. 235–236).

Nepal has few media resources of its own, and broadcast signals are hampered by the terrain, but still some things have been done. Educational radio broadcasting began in Nepal in 1956, and has continued to be one of the main sources of educational outreach in areas where teachers are few, or are overburdened by teaching more students at various levels (sometimes superseding even the availability of blackboards and chalk).

Bhutan

One of India's other neighbors is Bhutan (Drukyu) meaning "land of the Thunder Dragon." Situated in the Himalayas, bounded by China in the North and India on three sides, the rugged mountain territory has only 10% of the land that is cultivatable. Ten percent of the population live in urban areas.

Bhutan is a constitutional monarchy with a representative democracy. It has no political parties, trade unions, or formalized interests groups. All its communication passes through India, and the border with China has been closed since 1959. For this reason, India is an important neighbor and political relations are an important factor in domestic and trade relations. The largest concentration of population is in West Bhutan where the Dakupas live. Culturally and linguistically, they are related to the Tibetans. East Bhutan is inhabited by the Shersop Pa, who have links to the tribes of Assam and other neighboring states. In the south, the dominant language is Nepali, but official languages include English, Nepali, and Dronhag.

One of the most important factors for this nation is the per capita income, which is among the lowest in the world at approximately $80 per year. Of the labor force, 90% works in agriculture, and the literacy rate is extremely low at 10% (*Role of Adult Education and Mass Media for Civic Education*, 1985, Sept.).

Burma

Burma is a region with a difficult geographical problem; most of the population is divided into two regions, the lowlands, where the largest population (Burmans) live, and the hill areas, where the Shans, who migrated from southeast and inner Asia came from. These groups and other ethnic minorities retain the customs, language, historical, and political consciousness that shaped their regions.

Buddhism is a predominant influence on life and social customs, with Theravada Buddhism and the pre-eminent faith. There are also a number of Hindus and Moslems, and many Chins, Kachins, Karens, and some Christians. In some regions, Animist beliefs prevail.

Throughout the 1980s there has been a rapid development of telecommunications throughout Burma, financed largely by the World Bank (Bunge, 1983a). Most of the services through telephones, radio, and television are aimed at the urban areas; television broadcasts only during the evenings and on weekends.

The Research Policy Direction Board, a committee of Ministers has conducted the overall planning and coordination of scientific and technological research since 1965. The Board is supported by the Research Development and Coordination Committee, an advisory body composed of officials having competence in the various specialized fields of science, energy, and social sciences. The Union of Burma Applied Research, the Agricultural Research Institute, the Burma Medical Research Institute, and the Educational Research Bureau are the leading research institutes.

Networks of research are fairly well developed—others are establishments: the Atomic Energy Centers, the Geological Survey, Land Use Bureau,

Forestry Research Center, the Soil Mechanics Laboratory, the Housing Restoration Unit, the Instruments Center, and the Technical Information Center.

ASEAN AND PACIFIC RIM NATIONS

The areas in this section also share the experience of colonization by other countries, but in many cases also have had regional groupings that have merged formerly disparate cultures. The political exigencies of many of the ASEAN and Pacific Rim nations have created strange bedfellows of politics, tradition, and opportunities for influence (some good, some bad) from powerful nations and multinational firms.

At present, the ASEAN and Pacific Rim nations are considered by many to be the area for the greatest potential growth in the area of telecommunications. This perspective is in part due to the lack of unified communications and effective policies in the past, but also, partly due to the potential for major infrastructural development that is unhampered by earlier distribution systems that reflect financial investment in technology that would prevent new innovations. As a result, many problems of policy exist; blank tape production often facilitates pirated tapes at a lower cost than pre-recorded ones, and the ease of smuggling pre-recorded tapes *as* blanks makes control difficult. Trade between and among countries has created a relatively easy outlet for pirated tapes, primarily between Singapore and Thailand.

In addition, smuggled ethnotronic technologies have become increasingly available. VCRs make up the largest communication technologies for illegal trade, but televisions, audio devices, and to a lesser degree, microcomputers, are included in black-market trade.

Sri Lanka

After 145 years of British rule, the country of Ceylon became independent in 1948. Located only 18 miles off of the south-east tip of the Indian subcontinent, the region has a culture dominated by former British influence, and a social structure built on the caste system. The British Parliamentary system has been retained, and therefore elections every 5 years for seats influences which parties select the Prime Minister and Cabinet Ministers.

The two dominant groups, the Sinhalese and Tamils, are organized in different ways, and although the government does not officially recognize differences of caste, the influence of different social relations are obvious.

Sri Lanka has a very high rate of literacy (80%) and free education is compulsory for students between the ages of 5 and 14. Four universities train many of the people who will work in the largely agricultural economy, but also for advanced telecommunications training.

A ministry of research was established by the government in 1968 to consider problems related to the formulation of a national policy of science and scientific research. A National Science Council was also set up by an act of parliament to advise the Minister of Scientific Research regarding science, scientific research, and related issues (Nyrop et al., 1982).

The funding of large-scale telecommunications systems has often relied on arrangements with industrialized nations. Much of the current telephone system in the Colombo area of Sri Lanka has been developed in cooperation with Japan. Sri Lanka leases a transponder from Intelsat and operates a troposcatter system and a domestic system.

Malaysia

Malaysia is a country divided by sea, therefore it has several domestic problems of communication with which to contend. The nation became independent of Britain in 1957 as the Federation of Malaysia, but states on an island of Borneo joined the federation in 1963 and the name was then changed to Malaysia. A multi-ethnic nation, Islam is the official religion, but the Constitution guarantees a right to practice any religion, and every religious group has the right to manage their own affairs. Buddhism (both Chinese and Theravada), Confucianism, Taoism, Ancestor Worship, Hinduism, and Christianity all prevail.

The people represent large groups of Malays, Chinese, and Indians, and the people from the states of Sarawak and Sabah, from Borneo are indigenous. Malay is the official language, but English is used widely in business and government.

Malaysia has good intercity and international microwave networks. A submarine cable system linking Kuantan and Kuching opened in 1980, allowing direct dialing from the east and west regions (Bunge, 1984). Good telephone, telex, telegraph, mobile phone, and data transmissions are available, and by the end of October 1983, five exchanges were in place to facilitate regional communications. It was the first country of the region to adopt cellular mobile telephone technology, starting with the automatic telephone using radio (ATUR) introduced in 1985 as part of a plan to double the number of telephones in the region and develop the most modern telecommunications system in the area.

The British educational system remains, with 6 years of primary education and 5 years at the secondary level; in both levels, the study of English is compulsory. In 1980, 41% of the Malaysian Chinese and 61% of the Malaysian Indians were considered literate (Information Malaysia 1987 Yearbook, 1987), and the popularity of newspapers has been facilitated by four of the leading newspapers' computerization of operations. As early as 1984, BERNAMA, the Malaysian national news agency, computerized its operations.

Until 1970 the government was an overwhelmingly private sector econ-omy (Bunge, 1984), and in 1983 the government allowed the first private television network. Indigenous manufacture of color televisions began in 1989, although the technology came from the Sharp Electronics firm of Japan. The plan is to have all television sets in Malaysia produced domesti-cally by 1991 (*Asia Computer Weekly,* 1989).

In a controversial move, Malaysia began (on July 1, 1989) banning televi-sion advertisements that glorified a Western way of life. Furthermore, no commercials of scantily clad women in swimsuits or other unacceptable clothing are permitted, because consumer organizations and local academi-cians felt that the influence of foreign cultures on television was undermining Malaysian identity (*The Strait Times,* 1989).

Telecommunication Department operations were privatized in 1987, and all functions of the National Electricity Board and Telecommunication De-partment will undertake future development.

Radio and Television Malaysia (RTM) is used to communicate with rural areas and a sizable portion of the population has access to radio (71% in 1980, and 49% to TV in 1980). See Tables 5.3 and 5.4.

Indonesia

After three centuries of colonization by the Dutch, Western influence ushered in a class of urban intellectuals who became the elite and founded a national-ist movement that has fostered an attitude of accountability to both Islam and secular religions. The most predominant sect in the country are the Moslems, who comprise 90% of the population (Bunge, 1983b), although the majority are nominal adherents.

The area of Indonesia presents an interesting mixture of people; approxi-

TABLE 5.4
Televisions and VCRs (1985)

	TV	VCR, as % of sets
Bangladesh	300,000	.12
Cambodia	30,000	—
Indonesia	643,800	.17
Malaysia	1,051,272	22.20
Pakistan	130,000	.29
Sri Lanka	450,000	13.60
Thailand	500,000	13.51
Vietnam	—	.03
Burma	20,000	—
Phillipines	1,500,000	—

Source: UNESCO (1987b).

mately 300 groups consider themselves ethnically and linguistically distinct, and the culture has assimilated a number of Chinese, Arabs, and Indians. Many of the cultures have roots in island life that reassert traditional values. Although the social structure recognizes ethnic diversity, it is not uncommon to find sections of the social strata filled with similar cultures; for example, the greatest number of government officials trace their heritage to the island of Java.

Like many ASEAN nations, the influence of ethnotronic technologies and software has presented a new pattern of communication use:

There is an active black market in uncensored imported videotapes—first run-feature films and pornography. The government is trying to put a stop to the black market, but many elite audiences are quite matter of fact about the "door-to-door" video rental salesmen who arrive on a motorcycle with a black briefcase full of 50–75 titles, mostly abysmal in quality of reproduction-but of popular and relatively new films. (Ganley & Ganley, 1987, p. 136)

Indonesia and India were the first two countries in the area to cooperate in the use of a satellite for domestic purposes by signing a formal "memorandum of understanding" in January 1979 (Saksena, 1986). The coordination between India's INSAT and Indonesia's PALAPA satellites reflected the need to address problems of orbit frequency including the technical problems of frequency interference effects.

Education is an important factor in Indonesia. With a 60% literacy rate (Bunge, 1983b), the educational programs by means of distance education are considered high priorities. Even though postal services are available in 90% of the subdistricts, private courier systems are used to supplement the post in Indonesia to ensure the reliable and timely conveyance of audio and visual and printed teacher training materials to rural areas ("Information technologies," 1986). To further educational opportunities, a computer science center in Jakarta began to develop a computer network (UNInet) to link 44 state-owned institutions of higher learning, to promote cooperation in education, research, and administrative data processing. The implementation of the plan began in 1984 and was concluded in 1987.

Domestic satellite services relay two commercial satellite systems and 50 earth stations with 26 provisional capitals and 14 other points.

Thailand

The population in Thailand is distributed unevenly throughout the country, therefore educational radio has been used by the government since 1958–1959 as a means to help students "learn desired social values" (Tuladhar, 1986, p. 10) in areas where the number of teachers were not available to support education.

Thai media is relatively unrestricted by world standards in part due to the philosophy of responsibility lying within each individual (Bunge, 1981). Although the society reflects an ethnic and linguistic homogeneity uncharacteristic of ASEAN nations, the social system has recently experienced rapid change, particularly in urban areas.

The new social system reflects changes in status and power, although the elites are most represented by the military and upper bureaucracy. Religion (Buddhist) is reflected in the political system and is seen as a strong social and political determinant.

Laos

Bordered by Thailand, Burma, China, Vietnam, and Cambodia, Laos reflects a mixture of ethnic values. Although the official language is Laotian Tai, there are several other languages and dialects that make communication difficult. Historically, information had been passed orally from monks, boatmen, and tradesmen who linked towns and villages, and a strong sense of the importance of music (primarily ballads) remains.

Laos is one of the least developed countries in Indochina. Regarding telecommunications, the limited telephone service (established in 1967) serves primarily urban areas, although the radio facilities reach a good portion of the country through a network of eight stations. There is currently no television broadcast within the country, but signals drifting from Thailand are received.

As a poor country, Laos has been dependent on outside agencies and other industrialized countries for the upgrading of telecommunications facilities. In 1987 the World Bank and UNDP invested in upgrading the telephone system, so that now there is at least one telephone for every 485 persons (Whitaker et al., 1985).

Singapore

Since Singapore's independence in 1965 the country has been politically stable, and has progressed to the point of being considered a "newly developed country." With an economy improving since 1987, stability has increased, but the problems of development have also taken their toll.

Along with its changing culture, the nation has become a major center for pirated videocassettes and VCRs with a distribution system that reaches globally. Part of the new problems come from Singapore's status as a Free Trade Zone (FTZ) that encourages multinational production that offers major firms low (or no) taxes, low import/export tariffs, and low-paid, non-union workers. The results are mixed: More people work, but the low wages can be seen as further domination and exploitation of the masses.

The Singapore government has made the development of a software technology center for all Asian countries its primary goal. To do this, it has set up various expert boards to develop, promote, and coordinate the advancement of IT software and technology in the country.

Because of the economic interactions in the region, Singapore decided to embark upon a value-added technology-based and knowledge-based industrial strategy. The decision was based on the problem of exports becoming highly competitive, and also due to acute shortages of the labor force and limited resources. A high wage policy was adopted for encouraging mechanization and automation, and a new economic policy included program of upgrading the skill level of labor, encouraging research and development, and to speed up computer applications both in offices and factories.

The information technology planning committee was set up in 1980 by the government to plan for building computer expertise and for exporting software. Soon it was felt that the focus of the national computerization effort was too narrow, so the policy was modified to be more integrative of computer, telecommunication, and office system technologies (National Information Technology Plan, 1985). The plan recognized seven essential components:

1. development of information technology human resources by educational and skill programs to upgrade and train personnel;
2. development of IT culture through introducing and encouraging use within society;
3. development of an information communication infrastructure, to enhance investment by other countries and improve the social and economic life in Singapore;
4. applications of IT—in government, for efficiency, in training institutes, to train people in proper and creative uses of the technology, and to give tax incentives to companies for computerization;
5. nurturance of IT industries, including breaks for research and development;
6. fostering a climate for creativity and entrepreneurship; and
7. coordination and collaboration of the various sectors.

The South Pacific Islands

The South Pacific Islands include Papua/New Guinea, the Solomon Islands, Fiji, Western Samoa, and Tonga. In these countries the governments exercise sole control over ownership and the facilitation of all communication facilities, including print. Broadcasting (particularly radio) is given priority over television and print for funding and dissemination of information. It is the belief of many governments that radio alone can play an effective role in reaching the many individuals among the scattered islands.

Communication and transportation are huge problems for the region that covers a diversity of cultures, ethnic groups, languages. The poor conditions of mass communication in the region make it difficult for natives to know much about foreign news. Although some agencies exist to facilitate news such as OANA (Asia Pacific) and the Australian Associated Press (AAP), much of the information comes from external radio services such as the BBC and VOA (Abundo, 1985).

The use of satellites may be a significant aid to these countries, and Papua New Guinea has applied to the ITU for two orbital slots to facilitate both a C-band and Ku-band satellite. The future may see greater use of low-cost earth stations and fiber optics replacing costly transoceanic telephone cables (Jussawalla, in press).

THE INFORMATION SOCIETY MODEL

In the border nations of India the discrepant level of technological development presents an interesting focus for the information society and the development of information technology in these nations (see Fig. 5.1).

Nations such as Singapore, Hong Kong, Taiwan, and South Korea are centers of advanced technology for two reasons: First, they are the focus of advanced technology manufacturing and marketing for industrialized nations both for hardware and software goods and services (primarily because of cheap labor), and second because they gain economically by providing more work for more people. As nations with free trade zones, they attract multinationals that also effect the technology and social technology perspectives of the people in the nations.

Nepal, Bhutan, Sri Lanka, Mali, Laos, Burma, and Vietnam have very little indigenous technology development and are dependent on big neighbors like India, Pakistan, China, Australia, and Japan. Industrialized nations like the United States, the United Kingdom, Germany, and the United Nations agencies like UNDP, and the World Bank give assistance for setting up technology infrastructures and communication technologies per se, which may or may not be appropriate to the needs of these nations. Not only is there a technology dependence but there also is an economic dependence and need for regional assistance to get technologies; thus it limits the access to the technology. Moreover, because of limited resources, the technology is centered in urban areas, and rural areas are ignored.

Thailand, Malaysia, and Indonesia have some indigenous technology but they benefit by proximity to neighboring markets such as Singapore and Taiwan.

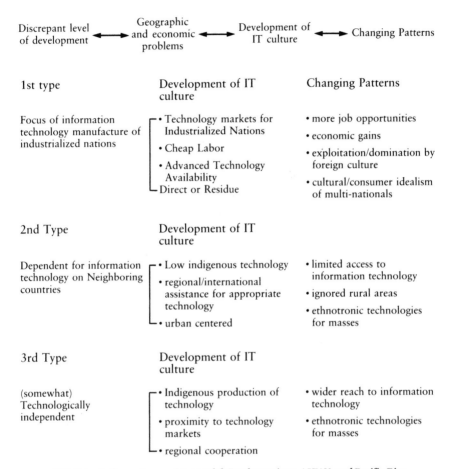

FIG. 5.1.   Information society model: Border nations, ASEAN, and Pacific Rim.

THE INFORMATION TECHNOLOGY MODEL

Among the nations in this chapter there is divergent technology progress and diffusion that pose many cultural challenges (see Fig. 5.2). A variety of factors such as traditions and customs, high population, illiteracy, cheap or exploited labor, and limited resources lead to development stress. There is economic and technological dependency for the diffusion of information

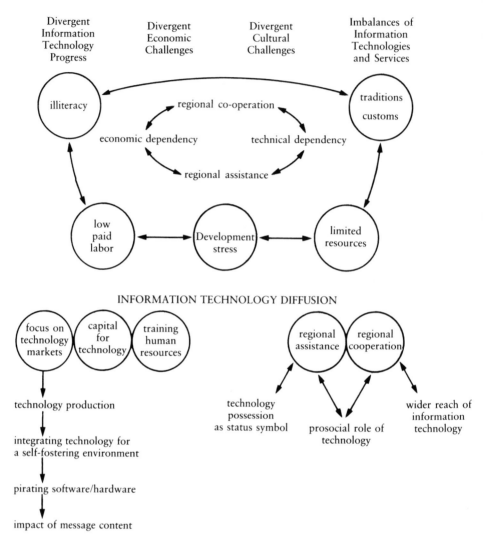

FIG. 5.2.   Information technology model: Border nations, ASEAN, and Pacific Rim.

technology, and because of such dependency regional assistance and regional cooperation is often a prerequisite for growth.

SUMMARY

The nations discussed in this chapter represent widely divergent rates of development. Each manifests a dependency on neighboring countries. In the area of telecommunications, the only hope for advancement may rely in part on developing programs of regional assistance.

Tradition plays a very important role in the development of each of these nations, and a tolerance for ethnic, linguistic, and religious diversity has contributed to social technologies that refuse (rightly so) to usher in change at the expense of tradition. In some cases, former colonization had affected traditions so greatly that remnants of colonial powers still appear and dominate political activity, yet in other cases, new political exigencies have created new countries from formerly geographically discrete communities.

It has been predicted that the ASEAN and Pacific Rim nations in particular may experience the information society more efficiently than any other region, because they are not hampered by former investments in infrastructures that will not keep pace with advancing information needs. These countries, dedicated to retaining traditional culture in the face of change, will undoubtedly be interesting to monitor as the world becomes tied together by technologies of communication. In doing so, they may well become the prototype of the information society.

Latin America: A Case Study

> The major paradox of technology with regard to information and
> communication favors concentration [of control] but risks marginal-
> izing the individual in society
>
> —Eduardo Vizer (1987)

The Latin American development experience has been overshadowed by the
location and power of the United States. Still, unique cultural and political
constraints have witnessed indigenous values and practices. The Latin American nations exemplify development in relation to extraordinary economic
constraints and political power structures.

This chapter explores the information technology policies and the development of domestic information industries in Latin American nations with
an emphasis on the three most technologically developed nations—Mexico,
Brazil, and Argentina. In many ways, these three nations share some common
background and concerns, but in each case, policy matters have been approached from distinctly different positions. The reasons for national policy
development in each country reflect an effort by each nation to either become
competitive in information technology on the global or at least national
scene, and address critical issues for developing countries, particularly in the
area of a nation's ability to control its destiny in the information age.
Argentina, Mexico, and Brazil all have attempted to become part of the
information societies with distinct approaches toward informatics and satellite distribution, with different rates of success.

This chapter also includes brief sketches of other Latin American nations,
but because they have expended development energies in areas other than

those of our central concern, they are kept brief. Although all of the Latin American nations have had to deal with issues of dependency, particularly because of their powerful U.S. neighbor to the north, the work of Cardoso and Faletto (1979) elucidates on some issues germane to Latin American nations. They insisted that particular situations need to be analyzed separately, rather than drawing on general theoretical models that are too rigid to explain the various peculiarities of these nations.

Still, Latin American nations do share some characteristics such as the predominance of Catholicism, huge rural communities, and for the most part, a common language, but the size of the nations, their economies, and their political histories are very different. Likewise, there are many similarities among Latin American values that are essential to understanding the systems of class, identity, and communication patterns that affect social technologies.

For example, Diaz-Bordenave (1976) has outlined the specifically Latin American relationship among large landowners and agricultural workers, which prohibits effective verbal communication and identification of common needs, the utility, and the effectiveness of change in adopting agricultural innovations. He enumerated the problems for communication and the adoption of new innovations thusly:

1. urban- and consumption-oriented communication sources,
2. communication channels weakly penetrating rural areas with irrelevant content,
3. farmers with limited decision-making power who are not organized or politicized,
4. inequality of economic capacity and differential access to information about innovations,
5. inadequate innovations,
6. oppressive rural social structure,
7. deficient infrastructure,
8. poor agricultural policies, and
9. geographical dispersion and isolation (pp. 50–51).

The work of Paulo Friere (1985) also addresses the need for an understanding of Latin American values that would effect changes in traditional practices. Friere's discussion of *conscientization* shows how education must be relevant to particular social groups for any change or development to occur. This position addresses the need for "cultural tools" that can be used to educate different social classes, including things such as appropriate forms of media, political groups, and a knowledge of present structures.

As nations with very large urban populations and concern for how information technology could enhance their respective economic status, Mexico, Brazil, and Argentina also share some other commonalities. In addition to the old, traditional cultures within each nation, extraordinary world debt situations, and historic class and political structures characterized by sometimes powerful military operations, and internal struggles between elite and worker classes, these three nations have all felt the domination at times by the United States. Since the 1920s, the United States has wielded power over each of these nations in the areas of technology transfer, media content, influence on foreign policy, and in some cases, through economic sanctions in the form of loans, political backing, or industrial ties. As these nations attempt to become newly industrialized countries (NICs), traditional associations with North American governments and firms are being questioned by political leaders often with the not-so-gentle prodding of the populace. Perhaps the fundamental question for these countries is then, whether internal manufacturing of information technologies and software can be effectively implemented without, or by limiting the dominance of other industrialized nations, at the risk of gearing up for technology that may be obsolete by the time the product is available to enter the market.

Two countries in particular—Mexico and Brazil—have surged ahead of other Latin American nations in telecommunications and IT development in the 20th century. In Mexico, the conscious decision to incorporate foreign capital in the informatics industries has permeated the rest of national development as well as influencing foreign policy. Brazil's decision to forego short- and medium-range productivity in order to concentrate on internal domestic development has concentrated on the strengthening of the infrastructures to support indigenous manufacture of telecommunications equipment—but at the cost of noncompetitive strategies for a period of time. Argentina's political and economic crises have thrown the development decisions from one side to another as the country first attempts to stabilize its domestic economy—but with incumbent political changes, the nation may have to address specific policy matters from a very different perspective than it has in the past.

SOUTH AND NORTH AMERICAN INDUSTRIAL TIES

Throughout the 20th century, Latin America was looked upon by dominant world powers as a haven for cultural domination. In the 1920s, RCA, ITT, Westinghouse, AT&T, and other U.S. industrial giants contributed to the development of radio systems through engineering, gifts of technology, and training of employees. After the world Depression and through WWII, a different set of priorities guided industrial development worldwide, and new economic allies were created with an eye toward eventual modernization and expansion.

By the 1960s, the dependency model was followed almost uniformly throughout Latin America due to the work of the Economic Commission on Latin America (ECLA), which conducted several prominent studies. Assumptions about how much technology (i.e., the number of telephones, type of transportation infrastructure, etc.) were viewed critically by the South as means of imperialism and control. Although many of these nations saw the influence of dominant countries as a necessity to growth, the partnerships were not entered into without the knowledge that these relationships would have a myriad of consequences for the nation itself.

Indeed, Latin America seems to have a hunger for media technologies, but suffers from limited economic resources. Radio covers close to 100% of the continent, but television and other telecommunication services (including postal services) are uneven. Various nations have grassroots programs to develop indigenous production of television and video content that speaks to the concerns of the people. For example, Chile produced approximately 200 documentary video productions between 1980 and 1984, analyzing poverty and unemployment. Although the nationwide broadcast of these materials may not be possible, there has been significant distribution to small groups of students, workers, grassroots organizations, and through other closed-circuit modes.

Computers are also spread unevenly throughout Latin America with the heaviest concentration (90%) to be found in the three most industrialized nations (Argentina, Mexico, and Brazil), which have limited domestic computer manufacturing facilities, although many parts are imported. Transnational firms like IBM, Digital, NCR, Burroughs, and Wang are heavily entrenched in the three nations, whereas all other nations must import all of their computer hardware. There is a tendency on the part of many authors to see the role of computer hardware as another case of imperialism or cultural dependency, but there may be more to the story than meets the eye.

Sarti (1981) has cautioned that many of the writings in cultural dependency theory have provided an illusion of what that means in Latin America. Indicating the subversion of cultural dependency themes, she explained:

Stressing the "passivity" of dominated societies some "cultural dependency" authors did not perceive that ideology is being produced *within* their own societies. This ideology serves the interests of the local bourgeoisie whose objectives are often so compatible with those of the hegemonic capitalist centers that a direct association between them develops. Furthermore, the local ruling classes are capable of dominating their own societies without the aid of instruction from abroad. (p. 327)

Thus, ideological dependency is related to technological dependency, but should be viewed with regard to how the political and technological structures in each society operate and function. As many of the Latin American nations began to exercise their own power, U.S. (and other foreign) presence became less popular. In many nations now, technological growth provided by the technologies made available through domination by a larger, more powerful nation are in a state of arrested development due to the nation's own ability to finance infrastructure maintenance and improvement. Like many nations of the world those of Latin America must decide to develop distribution systems for electronic communications from within, or, they must choose from whom, and how, to increase their present systems of communication. However, political upheavals throughout the 20th century have ordered priorities for the people of many nations. For the most part, this has resulted in the deterioration of several large technologies, but an increase in the availability of small technologies, in comparison.

A wide range of interpretations of political ideologies are represented throughout Latin America. Mexico, for example, meets formal criteria to be considered an authoritarian model, but the political system is clearly less authoritarian than in other countries that may also be considered authoritarian. Due to the constitution of 1917 and the Broadcasting Law of 1960, the Mexican government has the power to regulate all broadcasting, but there is considerable flexibility and freedom of the industries to operate autonomously, while in concert with the state.

Traditionally, throughout Latin America and as exemplified by institutions and organizations in Mexico, the concentration of control or power is in the hands of relatively few economically strong individuals, a system that has both created problems and has influenced the policies adapted by the government toward communication technologies.

Lipset and Solari (1967) have written that Latin America experiences political elites, military elites, religious elites, cultural elites, intellectual elites, and labor elites. In this sense, Latin America is not so different from other continental movements or identification of groups within countries, but throughout Latin America, these different elites groups have factioned themselves into political entities. The long tradition of elites in these societies has provided both traditional values that some think should be upheld (particularly those who are the elites), and major foci for societal reform (usually a position taken by those who have suffered under elite rule).

This contributes to the viewpoints of the disparate socioeconomic groups that are often further divided by geographic location. Huge divisions of urban and rural dwellers often generates a series of priorities that the urban and rural people can neither agree on, nor understand. In many cases, the geographic divisions then continue to exaccerbate divisions of rich and poor, powerful and powerless.

Concerns of the Masses

The elites seldom gave much credence to the concerns of the masses throughout Latin America until the various subcultures and classes began to assert themselves. In many cases throughout Latin America, as different political parties (including various interests of the military) exercised power, the political balance (or imbalance, as the case has been seen to swing radically from one political position to another). Although democracy is considered by many groups to be the dominant form of governmental organization in most of the Latin American countries at this time, it is rare to find a country that has not at some time in its history (often recent history) been dominated by an authoritarian government. In many of the countries of Latin America, the deep divisions of urban and rural, rich and poor, labor unions, peasants, elites, and other such groups, have often retarded the trajectory of development. The mere articulation of policy then, has become frought with political overtones, and the expense of investing in major communication infrastructures has been simultaneously effected by divided political powers, outlooks, and expenditures.

In many urban areas throughout Latin America, people have been politicized by working conditions, neighborhood identification, and other interests. Grassroots movements have been common throughout Latin America, but have often operated differently in specific nations. For example, in Brazil grassroots movements have less organization by social or economic class than in Argentina.

Citizenship, or identification with the nation, is also an issue. Whereas people in Argentina and Mexico have relatively great identification within the nation, other countries have comparatively little traditional social ties toward nationalism. Again, Brazil provides a point of contrast as it retains a variety of ethnic identities and suffers more from the "individuals living in Brazil" concept than the identification of the citizens as "Brazilians." This then, determines the citizens of a nation's reactions to the development of domestic industry, their willingness to live in an economically depressed or retarded condition, and more importantly, it addresses the issues of technology transfer, economic cooperation, and the gamble of weighing short-term versus long-term goals with major political consequences. Education is also another concern of the masses. Surprisingly, the statistics indicating the literacy rates in Latin America are high compared to other developing nations (see Table 6.1). This may be due in part to the emphasis of the value of

TABLE 6.1
Illiteracy in Latin America

Country	% illiterate	Year reported
Argentina	6.1	1980
Bolivia	38.6	1976
Brazil	25.5	1980
Chile	11.0	1970
Columbia	14.8	1981
Ecuador	19.8	1982
Mexico	25.8	1970
Nicaragua	42.5	1971
Paraguay	12.5	1982
Peru	18.1	1981
Uruguay	6.1	1975
Venezuela	15.3	1981

Source: UNESCO (1987).

education and of preparing oneself for active involvement in the political
events of a nation that come from Spanish heritage.

ARGENTINA

Whereas Mexico and Brazil have approached the growth of IT industries
from a perspective that incorporates greater use of IT by the governments
for its importance to domestic manufacturing, Argentina has been unable to
stimulate much development in the area of IT for primarily political reasons.
Within the study of Argentina, it is interesting to note how often the role of
government and the masses perspective have shifted due to the political party
in power as well as the problems of policies changing by new governments
in power. Because it provides such a composite of the Latin American
experience, we discuss Argentina's political history as well as the shifts in
policy planning and practice.

After 13 years of military rule that resulted in what has been called "the
dirty war," Argentina returned to a democratic system of governance in
1983. With a huge external debt and tremendous skepticism of government
on behalf of the people, the task of operating like a democracy has been
strained.

A large part of the political dialogue about telecommunication policies in
Argentina integrally relates *dependentista* and *anti-dependentista* sentiment.
According to Adler (1987), these beliefs stem from two conflicting interpreta-
tions of "progress:"

One has been represented by a loose coalition of conservative, laissez-faire-oriented landowners, industrialists, and financiers, supported by a significant segment of the armed forces. This coalition . . . sees Argentina's role in the international economic system to be that of provider for a hungry world and believes that industrialization is economically "bad" because it goes against Argentina's comparative advantages in cereals and meat and politically "bad" because it nurtures nationalist and populist movements, mainly Peronism. The other idea of progress has been represented by entrepreneurs of middle and small enterprises, labor leaders, some members of the urban middle class, the nationalists among the military, and the bulk of the Peronist movement, all of whom believe that Argentina's future lies only in industrialization and autonomy. (pp. 104–105)

The lack of a strong government with support by the masses has led the country to what Argentine Tomas Buch (1987) called "semi-development"—and he warned that countries of the South (particularly Argentina) may be "on their way to less development." An example might be a look at Argentina's budding electronics industry that once ranked as the "unchallenged number one" in Latin America (Rada, 1982), but because of political upheavals, now no longer exists as a possible player in Latin American domestic manufacture of ITs.

Since 1900, 13 Argentinian presidents have been removed by force. Various military coups have been enacted by different factions within the military. President Alfonsin (1983–1989) was the first democratically elected present to complete a term in office (6 years) in 64 years, and even he left office a few months before his successor took office due to political pressure. This political instability has created problems that can best be described through a brief history of Argentina's political connections in the 20th century.

A Brief History of Argentina in the 20th Century

Traditionally, the ruling elites of Argentina provided conflicting goals for development and international/national economic growth and stability within the nation. At the beginning of the 20th century power was held by the landowning elite (Conservatives) who had a policy of modernization for the country, but most of their own economic interests centered around agricultural and livestock exports to Europe. A growing middle class in the service sector, made up of European immigrants founded several political interest parties, such as the Radical Civil Union (UCR), which was marked by a desire to integrate the middle class, but had no specific platform or policy to attain this goal. The UCR was in power when the world entered the Great Depression of 1930 and the government's weak, inconsistent policies hurt both domestic production and external trade.

A military coup in 1930 seized power from the emerging parties and placed Conservatives in key positions—with a new focus on concentrating industrialization within Argentina. This action, however, was strongly derived from Spanish fascism, and the the Conservative Party itself, began to splinter into various groups, and the power of labor unions began to be heard.

Another military coup led by a special group of officers calling themselves the Grupo de Oficiales Unidos (GOU), took place in 1943. The GOU dissolved all political parties, suspended the Constitution, and divided the administration of government among their chosen members, one of whom was Colonel Juan Peron, who administered the Labor Department for the GOU, and went on to become one of the most powerful leaders in post-WWII Latin America. A brilliant politician, he amassed the backing of many of the working-class Argentines and also received backing from the Catholic Church. His Labor Party became known as the Justicalista Party—later to be renamed the Peronist Party. The Peronists also included an important youth group called the Montonerros.

Although Peron's policies of nationalizing industries in Argentina and investing in social programs for the poor and working classes were highly popular, the finances to upgrade certain infrastructures (such as telephones and transportation) were not available. Peron's policies incorporated social justice as the key element to national unity, and doctrine was "linked to an ideological characterization of Peronist Argentina as neither a capitalist nor a socialist country (a 'third-way' of development)" (Schnitman, 1984, p. 97). His use of the media to support his programs was part of his tremendous success in reaching the masses, and by 1950, Peron had seized state control of newspapers and broadcasting networks.

In 1955 a military coup deposed Peron and set up a government committed to replacing Peronist protectionism and encouraging anti-inflationary and developmentalist measures by adopting the economic plan of Raul Prebisch. In practice, however, only the former was enacted with the result "equivalent to dismantling the state protectionist structure benefiting local industry and reinstating foreign capital and agriculture as the basis of any future economic expansion" (Schnitman, 1979,[1] p. 147).

Dissatisfaction with these measures caused an unusual political alliance of the Peronist Party and a fraction of the UCR Party that elected President Frondizi in 1958. He was committed to nationalism and protectionism, but

---

[1]Schnitman (1984) has documented the growth of the Argentine film industry with specific reference to the types of protectionist policies invoked during several administrations, and his historical and contextual analysis of media institutions has provided an excellent base by which to measure the impact of other policy matters for media in Argentina.

was relatively weak and was coerced by the military into anti-inflationary plans that attracted foreign capital, particularly through Argentina's entrance into the International Monetary Fund (IMF).

The following Illia administration (1963–1966) tried to stimulate agricultural production, but what followed was an economic system that created more alienation between the industrialists and middle class. Once again this caused the pendulum to swing back to Peronist tendencies. In retaliation, the military dissolved all political parties, and sold many national firms to foreign investors, but during the years 1966 to 1973, specific groups in the military began to split between nationalist and liberal tendencies.

Peron returned to power in 1973 with a renewed commitment to raising wages and profits while maintaining social harmony, but old Peronist policies could not keep up with the inflation and change in the external debt. Peron died within a year of his return and his wife, Isabel, became president, although she functioned largely as a figurehead for military control. Her administration was marked by inflation rates of 600% and increasing debt, and when she was deposed by yet another military faction in 1976, the government stated that they would attempt to return to a "liberal, free market economy with emphasis upon increased foreign investment" (Snow, 1985, p. 14).

The military coup installed a system of government committed to putting an end to political disruption and achieving economic recovery. To do this the most severe measures were taken and according to Amnesty International, human rights abuses were among the highest in the world. For example, police cars were equipped with Digicon computer terminals that could read magnetic identity cards that gave instantaneous information of the person's history (Mattelart & Schmucler, 1985), and official statistics refer to 30,000 "disappeared persons," although unofficial figures put that total closer to 300,000. The military government's declaration of war with England over the Malvinas (Falkland) Islands in 1982 similarly resulted in a crisis of faith in the government but also bore witness to the power of communication. The military government declared war in an effort to create nationalism among the Argentine people and attempted to use print and broadcast media to convince the population that military victory was imminent, only to suffer one of the greatest defeats in Argentine history. When the BBC's external service announced the figures and declared a British victory, an incensed, disillusioned population called for a vote that saw the end of the military government and a shift to democratic government under the rule of UCR President Raul Alfonsin— a man who came to power as a representative of a party that had no economic plan, and who was forced to take take criminal action against former leaders for human rights abuses.

The Government Perspective(s)

When ENTEL, the telephone company, was developed in the 1920s with some domestic equipment manufactured in Argentina, and other equipment (primarily public telephones) purchased from Brazil, the purpose of telephony was to link the Conservative business people of Buenos Aires with the international networks for the furthering of agricultural trade. Landowning elite had less need to reach remote areas of Argentina, so the telephone system was primarily restricted to the major urban center enhancing the affluence of the urban areas and creating further distance from the rural people.

Other world events of the 1920s saw U.S. expansionism and exploitation of Latin America through other media such as the film industry and the development of radio. Like many Latin American nations, Argentina's radio system was introduced by U.S. firms like RCA, ITT, and Westinghouse, but these too were established primarily for the urban audience.

By 1930 a military coup wrested control from President Yrigoyen, who represented the growing middle class. Leadership was returned to the Conservatives who had a platform of "limited democracy," but financial considerations brought about limited state protectionism as a way of stimulating the domestic market. The policies as articulated by the government could not be instituted through practice due to more pressing economic matters, but some institutions were able to flourish, like the private radio and newspapers. With high levels of literacy and education, these media played an important role as organs of information for the population and they disseminated information about post-depression world agricultural markets and the high rates of unemployment in rural areas.

With a shift to greater internal production of goods, industrial Argentina began to flourish and even greater numbers of people left rural areas for urban, a change brought about and enhanced by radio and newspapers. These migrations put even greater strains on the telephone system as families desired to communicate with relatives still at home, and urban businesses and the need for support facilities grew.

By the time Juan Peron became president in 1946, the phone system was already too limited to accommodate the growing middle-class and urban workers. Former GOU policies of national control and a limit to external agreements had contributed to a growing feeling of nationalism in the country, particularly on the part of the working and middle classes and in the first 4 years of his administration, Peron seized on the nationalist sentiment and created policies of social change that poured money into social services. The ENTEL system was nationalized, but no resources were allocated to upgrade the infrastructure.

By 1950 protectionist measures had become more widely practiced than before. Peron's state control over media encouraged domestic content, but excluded outside interference. Criticism of the policies by many newspapers resulted in a strict censoring of issues, and in an effort to control information, Peron closed several newspapers (Alisky, 1981) and put further controls on radio.

Between 1950 and 1952 Peron's policies changed to even more restrictive measures, but a measure of political pluralism was retained. Although Peronism had begun with support from industrial workers, industrialists, and segments of the Army and Catholic Church, it ended in 1955 with "workers and the governmental bureaucracy . . . the regime's only supporters" (Schnitman, 1984, p. 123).

With unstable traditional media infrastructures in Argentina the world began to enter the "information age" with the development of computers and satellites. Argentina had effectively established domestic industrial activities, but had little to grow on in terms of continued development.

The military coup of 1955 brought in another agent in determining domestic production. Between 1960 and 1970 the military government sought to encourage foreign capital. Many of Argentina's domestic firms were sold to multinational corporations and the dependency debate heated up. By 1970 different political parties had split into various pro- and anti-dependentista camps. What followed was an attempt to generate a domestic computer market that would not only be competitive with world manufacturers in computer and microelectronics, but that would settle the debate about Argentina's future as an information-producing society.

The formation of the burgeoning computer industry in Argentina from the 1960s to the mid-1970s sets up an interesting comparison to those traditional media forms that had been established earlier in the country's history. Although the country had what seemed like all the right components to embark on domestic manufacture of mainframe and minicomputers, that is, a relatively diversified industrial infrastructure, high level of general education for the population, and scientific and technical expertise (Rada, 1982), lack of political support from elites during the last year of Peronist rule and the economic crisis caused the country to abort plans, even though a prototype computer had been successfully developed.

Although microelectronics were in their infancy in the early 1970s, the market was created to serve primarily urban facilities within the country, and excluded major export of microelectronics technologies. Part of the problem can be traced to the early 1960s at the University of Buenos Aires where research was conducted on electronic components, digitalization, and industrial electronics. The Ongania government's purge of "leftists" from the universities forced scientists from the universities and in many cases out of the country, while many went to work for multinational corporations or domestic electronics firms (Adler, 1987).

A private Argentine company called FATE, S.A. promoted the idea of domestic computer manufacture, and allowed Oscar Varsavsky (a Peronist supporter) to hire the best scientists possible. With a group of committed anti-dependency technicians and engineers, FATE initially focused on the calculator market and in a short time commanded more than half of Argentina's market, forcing their major competitor, Olivetti into serious trouble.

When the prototype computer was almost ready, members of the military (particularly the air force and members of the Instituto de Investigaciones Cientificas y Tecnicas) voiced interest in the project, but throughout the formative stages of the computer industry, two factions of the military began to emerge, one group with clearly more liberal tendencies, and the other committed to nationalist policies and practices.

From 1966 to 1973 the country had three other militarily installed presidents (Ongania, Levingston, Lanusse) and the conflicting policies and practices served to unite workers, students, and people from the rural areas. A return to Peronist rule in 1973 under Hector Campora was viewed as a return to antidependentista sentiment, and when Peron returned later that year, his old attitudes and policies were effected by the many changes in domestic and international economics.

After Peron's death and Isabel's exile by another faction of the military in 1976 the emphasis changed toward a desire for short-range economic efficiency, and a loan of $2.5 million needed by FATE to continue production was denied. In part, this denial was a measure of the anti-Peronist, anti-nationalist ideology of the new military rule.

Having effectively killed the possibility of domestic manufacture of computers, Argentina was not in a position to look to the use of computers on any major scale until 1986, when negotiations were made with Brazil to cooperate in an informatics project (Adler 1987).

The computer industry suffered from the clash of ideological policymakers who did not agree on whether the development of the industry could be maintained in an antidependentista (liberation) move, or co-opted by a rationalist perspective of integrating social forces. Conflicting interpretations by liberal and nationalist factions of the military specifically undermined policies that preceded them, particularly in an effort to abolish any Peronist power in such an important position.

When the military (government) acts as the interpreter of policy in a manner inconsistent with the originating policy makers, the entire infrastructural and productive components of the Sabato Triangle crumble. In this case, policies to encourage a domestic computer industry became the stepchild to differences in governmental (military faction) interpretations. The earliest military government had seen the function and structure of a domestic manufacturing of computers as a competitive edge toward gaining a place in the information age, and a useful activity for anti-dependency claims, but the 1976 military government regarded the activity as secondary to dealing with the economic crisis and felt that any move that would repress Peronist influence was more important than the domestic computer industry.

While the computer industry was struggling for life, television grew rapidly throughout Argentina. "Between 1959 and 1966, 22 privately owned and 4 state-owned television stations began to operate" and the diffusion of television sets through all socioeconomic strata paralleled the growing number of stations (Schnitman, 1984, p. 165). Originally, television was established to operate on the 525 line-scan technical standard, similar to the rest of Latin America and North America and a reflection of what equipment was most available to the area at the time.

Policy matters after the 1976 military coup, however, relied somewhat on reconstruction and speculation, because few records were kept during this period—some falsified—and others were destroyed. At best, we know that any official documentation for many communication technologies from 1976 to 1983 has been hidden from other parties' access (Robertson, personal communication, Sept. 25, 1987; Vizer, personal communication, June 18–28, 1986) and information is often difficult to corroborate. Specific development plans that were either announced formally or alluded to have often been found to be rumor or misinformation.

In an effort to control communications in and out of the country, the government restricted use of airwaves to use by the telephone company and to the military. The need for more and better telephone service has been a problem since the days of the growing middle class, but new switching devices and integrated circuits have been slow in adoption.

Mattelart and Schmucler (1985) wrote about an agreement signed with Nippon Electric (during the 1976–1983 military rule) for an optical fiber industry (and its relatives) involving the purchase of an optical fiber network that would replace the decaying cable system for telephony presently in use. According to the authors, the project was to be called the "Digital Ring of Buenos-Aires," but as of September 1987, no work on the development of this project had begun, and no plans had been made to institute them. The military government restricted use of satellite transmissions during 1976–1983. However, in the interest of denationalization and sharing in global information, the government did allow a LANDSAT earth station to be installed in Argentina during 1981 (the only other LANDSAT earth station in Latin America was installed in Brazil, in 1975). LANDSAT is a geological and meteorological remote sensing satellite—therefore, a LANDSAT base in the country was considered important primarily for monitoring the problems with the ozone layer in the southern-most regions of Argentina.

When the military took over from Isabel Peron in 1976, all radio and television stations were seized by the government and turned over to branches of the military for administration. The three private television stations in Buenos Aires were turned over to the Air Force (Channel 13), Navy, (Channel 11), and Army (Channel 9). These three television stations, along with the government-owned station (Channel 7) were directed to reduce the amount of foreign programming, and concentrate on Latin American (but primarily Argentine) content.

Although no records exist to explain why the military chose to change the entire television system from the U.S. technical standard of 525 NTSC to the 625 PAL system, speculation suggests that the U.S. system that needed significant updating was removed and the German system adopted because of a desire to (a) develop ties with German technology firms, and (b) reduce the availability of U.S. imports on the NTSC standard (Vizer, personal communication, June 18–28, 1986).

By instituting the only 625 PAL system in Latin America, however, other Latin American programs were also restricted. The costs of conversion from the 525-line scan to 625 were limited by the market forces, and even major exporters of Spanish programming, like Televisa of Mexico, or the Rede Globo Organization of Brazil, found it more expedient to concentrate on distribution for similar systems (see Table 6.2).

Ironically, the budget limitations imposed by the military also effected the nature of programming, and the costs of domestic production in highly inflationary times saw even a greater emphasis on imported programs—and an increase in U.S. series (Brennan, 1987), thereby serving to bring more North American (U.S.) programming to an audience that (according to the military) was to actively eliminate cultural imperialism dominated by the United States. The official government channel was to be used for primarily

TABLE 6.2
Radio and Television in Latin America per 1,000 inhabitants

Country	Radio Receivers		Television Receivers	
	1975	1985	1975	1985
Argentina	380	654	154	213
Bolivia	235	581	9	66
Brazil	157	391	—	184
Chile	164	332	68	145
Columbia	121	139	69	96
Ecuador	—	293	36	64
Mexico	—	190	—	108
Nicaragua	—	244	34	58
Paraguay	67	163	20	23
Peru	135	203	40	76
Uruguay	530	598	124	166
Venezuela	377	422	101	130

Source: UNESCO (1987).

political material, but this too backfired and became a public embarrassment: "Between 1977–1983, the Treasury loaned official television almost 53 million dollars (U.S.). . . . It lost 51 million" ("Cuanto Cuesta la Teve Oficial, 1987, p. 39).

The actions of governmental powers from 1955 until 1983, particularly influenced by various factions within the military and influenced by swings from military to Peronist tendencies, shows clearly how no policies toward communications technologies in Argentina could build on former policies. Furthermore, by treating communications as a "stepchild" problem, Argentina lost its advantage in electronics manufacturing and sacrificed the potential to become the dominant computer manufacturer in Latin America.

The problem of evaluating trends in past governmental policies toward communications technologies has also been seen differently by Argentine critics. Mallman (1987) has traced Argentine policy approaches through recurring cycles of political life based on "economic–technological" and "political–institutional" stages. Albornoz (1987) has outlined the influences of thought on the formation of policies that affect telecommunications technology and criticizes past policy directives as either integrating telecommunications development policies with education, economic, and industrial policies, or stressing compartmentalization that excludes adequate consideration of other public policies. These conglomerate policies have furthered either political aims or content aims (such as research and development), but he said that few policies have ever considered both avenues.

Ideas of the role of democracy and the functions of policymaking in a democratic government have been further discussed by Simpson Grinberg (1986) who cited Roncogliolo and Avila:

> Beyond the definition of communications there is a general social policy. And in this sense the central alternative is: authoritarianism or democracy . . . maybe it is time to stop proposing simply national policies of communication, in order to start designing policies of communications' democratization, with explicit adjective and purpose. (p. 163)

When President Alfonsin took office in 1983 he inherited an inflation rate of 400%, a level of unemployment approaching 25%, and a foreign debt perhaps the largest in the world in per capita terms ($44 billion U.S.) (World Bank, 1985). His platform promise included reform in the trade unions—a policy that was defeated by the Peronist majority in the Senate in 1984 (Graham-Yooll, 1985), but this action furthered his popularity among the "undecided" citizens (Vizer, personal communication, September, 1987).

In an interview with the editor of *South* magazine (Gauhar, 1984) he said:

> Our first task is to get the economy working again. We cannot pay the external debt in one day, and organize the economy overnight. We cannot do everything

at the same time. The majority of Argentines understand the situation better than some of the politicians. (pp. 24–25)

Although the Alfonsin government took a position of moving slowly and tackling the economy first, technological policy questions became the stepchild. Few new policies in the telecommunication sector were established, but new practices to encourage democratic operations were encouraged. In this case, democratic practices have preceded the creation of policy.

Although Argentina now has the second largest proportion of telephones to population in Latin America, with 11.2 telephones per 100 inhabitants, the telephone infrastructure is outmoded and costly. Lack of computerized switching devices (such as EPBX or ISDN switching systems) create spider-webs of wires hung above city streets, and old, mechanical switching systems are slow and inefficient. The 1987 cost to an Argentine for the installation and use of a telephone in the home or in a business setting was $1,500 (U.S.) because each facility needs a dedicated wire to connect with the trunk systems.

Although Argentina still has restrictive policies on the use of satellites left over from the military government, a working paper published in 1986 outlined the goals and benefits of increasing satellite usage through INTELSAT, INTERSPUTNIK, INTERCOSMOS, and INMARSAT (*Revista De Derecho Espacial,* 1986). The working paper was developed by a consortium of individuals under the auspices of the Faculty of Social Sciences at the University of Buenos Aires, and advocates the administration of all satellite policies be given to the Ministry of Culture and Information. In large part, the argument for increased satellite transmission capabilities was created to improve television and telephone facilities for a system of both national coverage, and regional program exchange (particularly with concern for educational television materials), and therefore, it was deemed appropriate to request guidance by the Ministry of Information and Culture.

When the restriction of satellite use for domestic communications is abolished, the nature of domestic communication could change rather dramatically. Alfonsin's attempts at cooperation with Brazil has foretold agreements that would allow Argentina to share transponder space on Brazil's satellite system. In anticipation of this agreement, many Argentines have loaded warehouses with (currently illegal) cellular telephone systems that would enable customers to bypass the wired ENTEL system and cost "only" $800, compared to the $1,500 ENTEL installation charge (Robertson, personal communication, Sept. 25, 1987).

When the civilian government returned in 1983, the television and radio stations were returned to the private sector. To encourage independent growth and development, President Alfonsin designated UCR members as "interventors"—or general managers—responsible for making the stations solvent again. The 44 radio stations returned to private control, and 72 new, commercial radio licenses were granted; while 10 new private television licenses were granted, all within 1983. By 1984, an additional 208 radio licenses and 8 more television licenses were granted with the promise of continued license expansion for both radio and TV (Dexter, 1987).

The establishment of so many new communication outlets for traditional television and radio also creates questions. Although the Alfonsin government advocated the granting of many licenses for enhancing local and regional identity, the number of persons with financial capital to support new systems were few. In some cases, a number of licenses are held by the same individuals or organizations, eliminating the local or regional content, and encouraging chain broadcasting or more purchased programming from other countries. A statute recommends that half of the programs on radio and television be Argentine in content, but this has been interpreted as advice and not law (Dexter, 1987). UCR policies toward privatization deny deregulation, but see privatization as the only viable means to keep expensive services from collapsing altogether. In this case, the government interprets policy with one view, but practice dictates another.

In an effort to improve the system of state television developed by the military from 1977 to 1983, government under Alfonsin continued to pour money into the official channel, but popular sentiment saw the development of this channel as one of "Alfonsin's follies" ("Cuanto Cuesta la Teve Oficial, 1987). Since 1983, state television has continued to lose money, although the rate of loss has decreased.

One democratic practice instituted by the Alfonsin government was the creation of organizations that function autonomously or semi-autonomously to bring together seemingly disparate groups to work together to solve problems that the government cannot effectively legislate.

Although some of these foundations are politically affiliated [i.e., the Fundacion for Communication and Democracy in Education (FUCADE), affiliated with the UCR Party], other have been established to bring political groups together, to work for common causes [i.e., Consejo Nacional Para Investigaciones Cienciticas y Technicas (CONICET) or the National Council for Scientific and Technological Research] was actually instituted in the first Peron era, but now uses a central mainframe database that, through its interest group, Groupo Esperanza, has begun to gather data to be used in the formation of socially relevant policies created to:

> organize and promote the involvement of academics, and promote the activities which deal with new technologies, institute new programs for the formation of disciplines critical to the development and modernization of the country, in direct connection with the investigation and specialization for the necessities of national and regional planning. (Mignone, 1987, p. 1)

A related problem, however, is the lack of office equipment—most notably minicomputers—to facilitate work with the CONICET data collection. A controversial plan underwritten with Brazil for cooperation in the field of computer applications in teaching (Mattelart & Schmucler, 1985) was announced but has started slowly and has not gained much momentum. A related problem involves the few terminals available for groups or organizations (in part, a problem of interfacing with telephone lines), and the University of Bariloche is the only university in the country with a full program in computer science (informatica).

Another significant development for policy formation was the role of the Ministry of Communication, closed since Peron's first administration (1943–1955). In 1985 the Alfonsin administration reinstituted a Ministry of Culture and Information, with subgroups including the secretary of science and technology, and the secretary of public information. The later also includes Undersecretaries of Social Science Research and Social Science Policy (Vizer, 1987).

After the military government took power in 1976, the role of universities and academic personnel in conducting research for the government was minimal. For a period of time, universities were closed and books destroyed. Since 1983 the universities have been opened to all Argentines (a policy of open enrollment has existed in most civilian administrations), and favor has been granted to the establishment of various research centers and foundations. Many of these institutes operate as "think tanks," sponsor students in universities within Argentina and outside; and solicit funds from outside agencies, like the UN, UNESCO, the EEC, or from private contributions.

A continuous problem for prior administration (from 1930 through today) has been the question of how involved Argentina should be with the more industrialized nations. While Alfonsin actively courted relationships with the United States (his visit to President Reagan in 1987) and Russia (Gorbachev's visit to Argentina in 1987), major contracts such as those reputed to be signed with Nippon Electric were avoided.

The Alfonsin government took a few steps to influence infrastructures or modes of production but it was not consistent in government's interpretation of its role as planner and facilitator, to the exclusion of any other traditional government interpretations. In the area of upgrading media infrastructures or production, the Alfonsin government was too limited by financial constraints to institute direct changes. By placing the economy as the overarching problem, policies that would require massive expenditures on the part of the government were placed low on the agenda, but democratic practices actually were instituted to make better use of existing facilities. In doing so, the Alfonsin government provided a lesson for other developing democratic societies, in that practice could effectively precede policies.

The Masses Perspective

Obviously, in the case of Argentina, there have been times in history in which the masses had greater input into the formation and execution of policy. However, when a great number share a history in which they seemingly have been lied to or "sold out" by government, a tremendous skepticism about the possibility for development exists.

Similarly exorbitant duty fees (i.e., $2,000 U.S. for a minicomputer or $200 for a manual typewriter) make personal electronic technologies items only for the privileged. A $50 package of video games may cost an Argentine $200 if purchased in the country, or an additional $50 if brought in from outside. Therefore, items like telephones or goods that might interface with large communications infrastructures rarely make their way legally into the country (see Table 6.3).

MEXICO

The Government Perspective

Mexico has forged a unique policy toward developing an IT infrastructure by a system that has created an alliance for research in this area between government, private industry, and universities.

An example of the type of media policy that preceded the present IT policy would be the government's realignment of traditional broadcast facilities and

TABLE 6.3
VCR and Television Penetration in Latin America

| Country | 1983 | |
	TV sets in use	VCRs as % of TV sets
Argentina	6,000,000	.73
Brazil	22,000,000	.39
Chile	1,325,000	2.09
Columbia	1,750,000	.09
Ecuador	500,000	.09
Mexico	8,500,000	.53
Paraguay	350,000	.67
Peru	1,364,933	.28
Uruguay	350,000	.38
Venezuela	1,710,000	11.14

Source: UNESCO (1987).

culture industries. The most dominant broadcasting group in Mexico is *Televisa*, which was formed in January 1973, by the merging of two private commercial television companies, Telesistema Mexicana (TSM) and Television Independiente de Mexico (TIM). Televisa is accountable to both the Ministry of Communications and Transport (SCT), which controls licensing and technical components of broadcast regulation, and the Ministry of the Interior, which exercises authority through the General Directorate of Radio, Television, and Cinema (RTC). The RTC regulates content and authorizes the production of content for the government stations. (Mahan, 1985). This restructuring has been viewed as a precedent and a model for growth in other technology areas in the country.

For many years, the government of Mexico facilitated no construction of an indigenous IT industry, but in recent years, "Mexico has become the second largest producer and consumer of computers in Latin America" (Miller, 1986, p. 173). Although other Latin American nations (like Brazil) have found it necessary to close their economies to foreign competition, Mexico has been taking greater steps toward liberalizing industrial trade since 1985. American, European, and Japanese firms have invested heavily in the Mexican economy. This has also helped to increase the country's ability to develop indigenous industry.

Certainly, Mexico's sharing of a geographical border with the United States has influenced the development of technology within Mexico, and has also had an impact on the Mexican government's ability to develop policies without external pressure from the north. The proximity of the United States has influenced Mexico in three ways:

1. As a heavy investor in Mexico's economy, the United States tends to overshadow and influence internal policies as well as trade policies. Because the United States has invested so heavily, the Mexican economy the the development of foreign policy is also subject to the vicissitudes of the United States and international economic markets.

2. The technological advantages of the United States and the investment capital in Mexico significantly affects technology transfer.

3. The United States has virtually no formal foreign policy with regard to trade with Mexico.

What these factors indicate, is that Mexico is undoubtedly overshadowed by the interests and whims of the United States. A case in point would the U.S. leverage in forcing Mexico to liberalize domestic trade policy and join the General Agreement on Trade and Tariffs (GATT). When Mexico wanted to offer incentives to attract foreign firms, such as tax credits and special energy fees, the United States cried that such incentives would violate GATT code and give Mexican informatics producers an unfair advantage in international trade (Miller, 1986).

Mexico's huge foreign debt has influenced technological development and telecommunications policy in recent years. The debt crisis is also a major factor of the masses' concerns regarding the adaptation of small technology. For example, since 1982 the Mexican government has devalued the peso several times, including a devaluation in 1985 that exceeded the inflation rate.

These economic imperatives have reduced the willingness of foreign capital to invest in Mexico, but in part, have also aided in the prioritizing of industrial issues. In the past, Mexico has acted as the labor pool for foreign firms in informatics that have sent components into the country, and then have exported them to other countries. Major players in this arena are ITT, Indetel, GTE, and Telendustria Ericsson (of Sweden). From West Germany, the Siemens Corporation has dominated the manufacture of telex equipment.

Mexico has begun to concentrate on computer technologies and peripherals to the exclusion of other telecommunication manufacture, although they did increase production of televisions, stereos, radios, and other audio equipment in the 1970s, with a concentration on creating the components for these technologies domestically.

The real emphasis for Mexico, however, has been in the area of computers. Although the size of the market is only about 33% – 50% the size of Brazil's market, and a mere 20% of the U.S. market, the growth of the industry in the 1980s has been noteworthy. Prior to 1981, virtually all computers in the country were imported, but since the Computer Decree of 1981, which took effect in 1983, efforts have been made to cooperate with foreign industry, academe, and government in the research and development phases of computer manufacture and peripherals, which extend to the manufacture of duplicating machines, typewriters, and other electronic office equipment.

To ensure the development of the domestic market, Mexico has also set content quotas, import and export quotas, and has enacted a Foreign Investment Law that limits outside firms from owning more than 49% of any manufacturing operation. However, exceptions have been made in the case of the U.S.'s Hewlett-Packard and IBM industries, to encourage the manufacture of minicomputers.

Mexico launched its first satellite (MORELOS 1) in June 1985, and MORELOS 2 in November 1985. The first satellite extended coverage nationwide, and the second enhanced services to one third of the population that had few information resources.

The Masses Perspective

A dominant concern by all people in Latin America is the economy, and in most cases, the outrageous national debts that influence wages, prices, and taxes. As in all desperate economies, the greatest taxes are levied on imported luxury goods. In many cases, these goods are small, electronic media such as watches, microwave ovens, television receivers, VCRs, computers, and so-called "fancy phones." Outrageously high duty rates then, have encouraged the smuggling of small technologies in particular, over many borders:

> Almost all the Sony products available in Mexico have been smuggled in. At places like Mexico City's Tepito market, as well as at legions of smaller retailers, black-market consumer goods ranging from food processors to satellite earth stations are readily available. Indeed, a substantial percentage of the stock at almost any retail electronics outlet in Mexico is contraband. The U.S. headquarters for most major brands—including TDK, Memorex, Sanyo, Pioneer, Fuji, as well as Sony—cannot point to a legal channel of distribution within Mexico, yet their products are readily available, and in some cases are even advertised there. (Weinstock, 1982, pp. 95–96)

Ironically, although the stopping-off points for smugglers bringing electronic goods into Mexico necessitates smuggling over the U.S. border, most of the goods are manufactured in Japan, the reason, according to Michiaki Ina, the former editor of the Japanese magazine, *Economic Monthly,* being that U.S. firms are more profit oriented, whereas Japanese firms are more volume oriented (Weinstock, 1982).

These practical concerns for the members of Latin American nations then, complicate the acceptance of expenditures in large-scale IT industries and become a cultural concern for policymakers throughout the nations.

BRAZIL

Brazil is a country that is considered a democracy, although like other Latin American democracies, the move to this form of government was not a peaceful transition. In the second half of the 1970s the military government in power in Brazil began to promote liberalization while popular movements throughout the country began to grow (primarily centralized in the urban areas).

Between 1980 and 1984, Brazil had the lengthiest and worst economic crisis in recorded history. Ironically, this period of time coincided with the government's plan to forego economic efficiency in short- and medium-range timeframes to stimulate national firms to attain mastery in manufacturing and designing data-processing systems.

The Government Perspective

Brazil's entry into the IT arena can be traced back to 1968, when the government set as its goal the enhancement of science and technology as a major growth area. Similarly, the Navy was extremely interested in self-sufficiency in hardware for the outfitting of naval vessels, and an interest by the private and public sector in the area of information technologies enhanced the development of the domestic IT manufacturers.

In 1972, a computer council (CAPRE) was founded to prevent unnecessary imports and increase the efficiency of data-processing equipment for the Brazilian government (Frischtak, 1986). As a forerunner to the Secretaria Especial de Informatica (SEI, established in 1979), CAPRE was the body responsible for the issues of technology transfer, foreign investment, domestic planning for research, development, and growth of the industries and policy.

Frischtak summarized the goals of industrial policy for IT in Brazil:

> among its general objectives are to maximize the amount of information resources located in Brazil, no matter if produced in Brazil or imported; to assure the national control over their production, implying that the main decisions related to data industries are made in Brazil and that their technologies are mastered by national firms; to universalize access to information; and to use information resources as a key instrument for the enhancement of the cultural and political environment in Brazil. (pp. 39–40)

The National Informatics Policy Law, which went into effect in October 1984, further stipulates the requirements for indigenous manufacturing and production. The goal is to stimulate the country's ability to be self-sufficient, but secondarily to form the nucleus of Latin American exports in telecommunications equipment.

The government has, like Mexico, ceded the necessity of foreign capital participation in enhancing state and national goals, but Brazil has also begun to stimulate internal brainpower by investing in colleges and universities that would promote education in science and technology. Trained personnel in these areas increased almost three times between 1974 and 1978 (Frischtak, 1986). The result has been that informatics manufacturing in Latin America is dominated by Brazil, with the exception of the global giant, IBM. Still, until 1975, Brazil relied heavily on computer imports for its growing information development areas. Between 1975 and 1983 it has grown to:

> between seventh and eleventh in the world computer market. The Brazilian market [then equaled] about one-fifth of the German, one-quarter of the British and French, and half the Italian market for computer products. However, the sale of computer products in Brazil (was) growing faster than in these countries. (Tigre, 1983, p. 44)

A large part of the domestically produced medium to large computers facilitate government work, including state and municipal activities. The large banking sector in Brazil also makes heavy use of mainframe and minis, including intelligent terminals.

The role of the multinationals (MNCs) in Brazil cannot be overlooked. Although some specifically Brazilian developments in computer manufacture have been created through government and university cooperation, the financial cushions provided by the vast number of MNCs operating in Brazil have stimulated cooperation and have been viewed as necessities. Although the Brazilian goal is to excel in domestic research and development, this would have been impossible without the technology transfer, engineering knowledge, and money supplied by foreign investment.

What has emerged, therefore, is an innovative licensing policy that has been considered to provide more competition in the informatics industries. Second, this policy has been cited to help develop product or process design in an environment where technical support was still weak (Tigre, 1983).

Although Brazil is similar to Mexico in an acknowledgment of the need for foreign capital, experience, and manufacturing, the notion of quotas and eventual give backs are more closely followed in Mexico than in Brazil, where the size of the market allows for more culturally relevant concerns to dictate policy and speed domestic manufacturing. Although Mexico's policies favor a gradual expansion of the domestic market and a downplay of foreign capital investment, Brazil sees limited multinational involvement as an opportunity to stimulate competition and cooperation at a different level, which emphasizes domestic research and development. To reduce the debt, the Brazilian government has experimented with a program to exchange part of the debt for equity in Brazilian enterprises. Debts have been auctioned off at discounts of 26.5% and 27% for every $100 of debt exchanged, which then enables creditors to be entitled to approximately $73 of Brazilian property, most of which is in the Amazon Basin (Investing in Brazil, p. A3, 1987).

The Brazilian government also introduced the Cruzado Plan (February 28, 1986) to attempt to bring inflation to zero. Inflation rates over the years have seen the following increases (*Handbook of National Development Plans,* vol. 1, vol. 2, 1988):

1982: 98%
1983: 142%
1984: 196.7%
1985: 400%

The Masses Perspective

A serious problem in Brazil stems from the diverse geographic separation of urban and rural peoples, as well as a class system that reflects both political and ethnic diversity. Many of the government plans to stimulate IT industries have required geographic relocation of classes and groups of people to parts of the country that challenge their historical beliefs and value systems.

For example, the country moved it's capital of Rio de Janeiro to Brazilia—which was founded for the express purpose of relocating government workers and support staff from the crowded urban area to one that would provide a new start in terms of controlling for transportation, housing, and so on. The construction of Brazilia, located deep in the jungle, presented many obstacles and impediments to the effective operation of government, but socially, the relocation of a great number of people and the information needs of the people and the government were greatly stressed.

As in Mexico, the pragmatic concerns of the masses focus on the day-to-day need for communication and information, locations for work opportunities, and fair wages. Along with these concerns are desires to use small media, obtained at reasonable prices and legally, to contribute to a sense of social identity.

The need for cultural affiliation and integration is often enhanced when geographic relocation takes place. In some ways, the televised offerings by the huge *Rede Globo* corporation have eased transitions and brought national economic concerns into the homes of Brazilians through fictionalized programs (soap operas, made-for-TV films, etc.), and through news and information programs that have brought the government's goals and aims into the homes or viewing environments of the masses. The Globo television network covers 95% of the 17 million households, and the Globo organization also produces a daily newspaper, 30 radio networks, a major record company, and a home video division.

TRADITIONAL GOVERNMENTAL APPROACHES
TO IT POLICIES IN LATIN AMERICA

When policies toward communication technologies are treated as stepchildren rather than major foci, they remain weak and mitigate against democratic principles that reflect a desire to represent the people of the nation. Domestic stability has much to do with the willingness of the public to adhere to governmental policies, and by facilitating personal technologies on a level that more of the population can afford, the government supports *some* satisfaction with life and serves to limit black-market or other illegal practices.

The conservative Mexican, Octavio Paz (1983) wrote:

Latin American democracy arrived late and has been disfigured and betrayed once and again. It has been weak, undecided, revolted, it has been its own worst enemy, a victim to the adulation of the demagogue, corrupted by cash, undermined by favouritism and nepotism. And yet, everything good that has been achieved in Latin America, since a century and a half ago, has been done during, or on the way to democracy. (p. 188)

In addition to the political exigencies, the majority of development policies in Latin America since the 1970s have dealt with issues of debt. In some countries national development plans have tended to envision telecommunications development as a way of getting information to the masses, and therefore have elevated telecommunications infrastructure improvements to primary goals.

LATIN AMERICA AND THE CULTURAL CONTEXTS

Regional Cooperations

Satellites. INTELSAT provides the transponders for services to a number of Latin American nations, including Argentina, Brazil, Columbia, Chile, Peru, Mexico, Panama, Uruguay, and Venezuela. However, specific projects for education and development using regional satellite distribution came through the SERLA project (1971 – 1974), which distributed Spanish educational materials to a number of nations with receiving stations.

The first Latin American nation to have its own satellite system was Brazil and the BRASILSAT system (1985). Mexico launched its MORELOS satellite system later in 1985, as an effort to combat problems in communicating to the one third of the population that still has no access to communications.

Other systems have been proposed, but have not yet been implemented because of financing or other such constraints. The most notable of these is the CONDOR system suggested by the five Andean nations.

Specific National Plans

In many nations of Latin America, specific development policies have been proposed by governments in power. The brief sketches here indicate government perspectives for development through telecommunications, and also indicate the government's acknowledgment of social technologies as a component to integrated change.

Bolivia. Bolivian radio is controlled by the state, and television was started in 1969 as a monopoly by Television Boliviana. Unauthorized private television exists in some areas, and spill from other countries is predominant. The government of Bolivia has no formal censorship programs for any of the media, but the Bolivian Press Law states that news and information should be from an acredited source.

Chile. Chile has arranged for a system of public investment in telecommunications, and has had a steady increase in the financing of an infrastructure that would support greater regional development (*Handbook of National Development Plans,* 1988). From 1982 through 1984, the investment in the telecommunications sector rose by $10 million (U.S.) a year.

A 1980 statistic indicates that microcomputers in Chile account for 75.9% of the computer market, a figure much higher than most of the informatics technologies in Latin America, and similar only to Brazil's interest in micros compared to larger mainframe or supercomputers (NCT/NCT Newsletter, 1986).

Chile has both government and private radio and television stations, and a large number of newspapers (37 dailies), with the Santiago having as many as 10 daily newspapers (Kurian, 1987).

Columbia. Columbia has the smallest per capita external debt of any other Latin American nation. Columbia's internal communication needs call for the establishment of greater power networks to support electronic technologies. The National Development Plan of 1981–1984 called attention to the need to increase telephone and telecommunication infrastructures, and there has been an increase in the manufacturing of domestic telephone receivers.

Columbia has had television since 1954 through INRAVISION, administered by the National Institute of Radio and Television. The two official channels reach 85% of the population, with one channel exclusively devoted to education. Chile is also increasing television programming through pay systems on UHF. Four channels will be distributed via satellite and supported by advertising, and it is interesting to note that the sole content of the fourth channel will be telenovelas (soap operas).

Ecuador. Like Mexico, Ecuador has attempted to integrate social policies with technological and economic development policies. The emphasis is on rural communication structures, education, health, and housing; but Ecuador specifically states that a concern for different cultures within the nation must guide development plans.

The development plans of 1980–1984 specifically focused on transportation and further development of policies that consider technology transfer from outside the country.

Venezuela. The development plan of Venezuela specifically states that "the central goal of the long-term strategy is to advance toward the establishment of a more democratic and more egalitarian society" (Handbook of

National Development Plans, vol. 2, 1988, p. 407). Official planning for development in Venezuela started with the Oficina Central de Coordinacion y Planificacion de la Presidencia de la Republica, in 1959. While the fifth plan (1976–1980) called for heavy industrial growth, the sixth plan (1981– 1985) emphasized social sectors, including housing, health, education, and nutrition.

To further social technologies, the government plans to consolidate the democratic system by focusing attention through development plans on the following:

- the 0 to 6-year-old child;
- the protection of women legally;
- the development of care for the aged;
- the support of cooperatives, trade unions, and so on;
- the cooperation with other developing countries; and
- the diminishing of interregional disparities in income and employment.

Peru

Another country that has developed a sophisticated plan toward telecommunication infrastructure enhancement is Peru, which plans to do so by attracting foreign investments and restructuring the foreign debt. Peru's plans to increase power and telecommunications brings in a specific plan:

- public investment in telephone extensions (Phase II),
- rural telecommunication program (Phase III),
- National data transmission plan,
- expansion of a microwave network,
- development of a north-to-east microwave system,
- expansion of the microwave system for Arequipa-Lima-Trujillo, and
- establishment of a rural telephone exchange system.

In part, this enhancement of a telematic infrastructure has to do with the domestic manufacturing of microcomputers by Peru, although the market for domestic and export use is still extremely small and is overshadowed by North American production.

THE INFORMATION TECHNOLOGY MODEL

If it is possible to indicate a generic model of information technology in Latin American countries, it must focus mainly on political power. The diffusion of information is mainly at the elite level, and the information trickles down haphazardly to the marginal masses although they are not the major focus.

The major components of the model are foreign policy and political ideology that has traditionally culminated in technological domination by foreign powers, often through economic leverage. But the resulting cultures and ideological positions have witnessed dependency on a wider scale, and one should not assume that the political structures within each nation were ideologically neutral prior to the technological development provided by other forms of domination.

Information technology suggests three considerations; first, the technology transfer by inviting foreign capital for industrial ties with political backing; second, the focus on media content that may be directed by conglomerate policies; and third, the focus on foreign policies that aim at attracting foreign capital and economic cooperation (see Fig. 6.1).

When these three major foci are put into operation, the outcome could be either an information technology crisis or the development of the information technology industries. A crisis occurs when there is political, economic, or cultural instability. The political crisis may be due to political instability, military coups, and political factions. The economic crisis may result in economic dependency, thus making the information technologies expensive and unavailable. The cultural crisis will not only result in cultural dependency but may erode cultural values. If the development of information technology industries occurs, then there will be increased communication and information links, increased work opportunities, and an increased capacity to earn.

THE INFORMATION SOCIETY MODEL

The input resources of information culture can change patterns of information technology as well as the information environment. In this context, there is a variation within Latin American countries such as Mexico, Brazil, and Argentina (see Fig. 6.2).

Mexico: The IT culture resources of media policies, government perspectives, perspective of the private industries, and the academic perspective change the patterns of broadcast facilities and development.

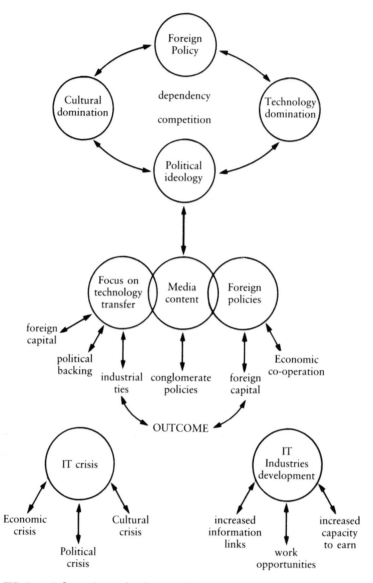

FIG. 6.1. Information technology model: Latin America.

Brazil: The IT culture resources of national government control, indigenous production, and being the nucleus of Latin American exports can
enhance cultural and political environments and attract foreign investment and technology.

Argentina: The changing patterns of political and economic instability

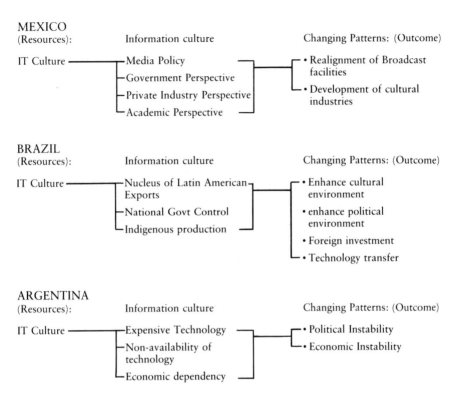

FIG. 6.2.   Information society model: Latin America.

will effect the information environment by making information technologies expensive and unavailable and will also lead to greater economic
dependency.

SUMMARY

Latin American nations have experienced many forms of domination—
political, technological, cultural, and most important in recent times, economic. Although many of the nations share a common language, internal
systems of society have established different criteria and needs for social
development.

The three countries we have focused on more specifically have found that the system of elites and political power in each nation has influenced what policies would be considered for growth in an information society. It is obvious that no policies can speak for both the government and masses perspectives; but that the aims and goals of each create a different set of priorities that the other cannot completely ignore as they move to more democratic systems of governance.

The problems of Latin American nations will never be completely solved, but through regional cooperation and an increasing attempt at coordination with each other, a truly Latin American perspective in the information society may emerge. Unfortunately, problems of domination from wealthier countries have been seen in some cases as less of a problem than nondevelopment. The creative, yet complex means of financing national development in technological systems may yet show a different path to development; but the concerns of the masses and the attention to social technologies does not seem to be part of the future scenario—at least at this time.

Arab Nations: A Case Study

You want to know about telecommunications in Saudi Arabia? Easy.
Whatever the King says, goes.
  —Daniel J. Bardy (personal communication, October 18, 1988)

The importance of tradition in Arab nations provides the fundamental key
to understanding what development priorities have been deemed important
by nations and groups of nations. It is tradition, Islam, and the common
Arabic language that has united countries in the Middle East and the north of
Africa. The countries that constitute the Arab world are sometimes grouped
differently by some authors, but the criteria used to discuss these nations in
this chapter include the religious, historic, and ethnic boundaries. The area
for discussion then, includes Algeria, Liberia, Egypt, the Sudan, Lebanon,
Syria, Jordan, North Yemen and South Yemen, Iraq, Kuwait, Saudi Arabia,
Bahrain, Quatar, the United Arab Emirates, Oman, Algeria, Libya, Morocco,
and Tunisia. The countries of the United Arab Emirates (federated in 1971)
include Abu Dhabi, Dubai, Sharjah, Ras al-Khaimah, Fujairah, Umm al
Qaiwain, and Ajman. Not all countries are discussed in depth; rather, the
unique characteristics that support the research questions of this book are
addressed as appropriate in representative countries. Because Islam is the
unifying theme in this chapter, we also include Iran, which is often classified
along with Arab nations of the Middle East by several international agencies.
    The extraordinary financial resource provided by oil reserves in some of
the Arab nations enabled relatively undeveloped nations to propel themselves
toward an information society with virtually no economic restraints after
1973–1974. By no means less important than the economic shift has been
the dominance of Islam and the impact of that religion on social practices
has affected social technologies. The Arab nations reflect highly stratified

129

populations based on class, tribal affiliation, and religious beliefs; and Islam
dictates that religion and state law are synonymous with governmental policy
goals.

Islam provides a social system. There is no hierarchy of the church to
mediate between God and the Faithful; rather, each male Muslim is equal
in helping articulate the *ijma,* or concensus will of the people (Mansfield,
1985). Social practices may indeed change, but the change is usually slowly
adopted by public opinion. Obviously, the speed afforded by modern technologies challenges traditional practices; therefore governments have had to
regard information technologies as threats to traditional practices, thoughts,
and social relations.

Although there have been attempts to forge a union among Arab nations
for specific economic, political, ideological, and cultural reasons, such as the
Syrian–Egyptian merger of 1958–1961, the Syrian–Iraqi–Egyptian merger
of 1963; Libya, Sudan, and Egypt, 1969; the Syrian–Libyan federation,
1979; and the unification of the two Yemens, October 1972, what has
emerged is a return to fundamental beliefs that sets the Arab nations apart
from most other developing regions. Mansfield (1985) has written the
following:

> Thirty years ago Arab nationalism in the sense of a political pan-Arab move-
> ment was regarded as the driving force in the Middle East. Today it is often
> declared to have perished, to be replaced by the more fashionable movement
> of Islamic revival. (p. 468)

Therefore, as we discuss the use of technologies and social movements
within individual Arab nations and as treated in the aggregate, we must
necessarily view developments within their contemporary cultural contexts—which include many years of colonial intervention in some nations,
but little in others; wide fluctuations of GNP and petrodollars in some
nations, but not in others; direct contact with the industrialized world in
some cases, but a choice to restrain from outside influence in some others.
The result then, is a group of nations with individual financial and social
investments in the information society, but links to traditional society that
may likewise challenge the ability of western scholars to fully understand
the dynamics. Actions in recent years, such as the Ayatollah Khomeini's
death threat to author Salman Rushdie, was considered an act of barbarism
by the west, but the meaning of the act has more culturally aligned consequences.

> The worldwide conviction that the Arabs are incapable of settling their internal
> differences and will always indulge in passionate mutual recrimination remains
> deeply rooted. Certainly they have given good grounds for this belief in recent

years. One of the reasons, as we have seen, is that the myth of the unity of the Arab nation is at once so powerful and so idealized that some degree of disillusion is inevitable. Yet if the Arabs have a capacity for quarreling they also have a great talent for reconciliation. The spectacle of Arab leaders embracing only days after denouncing each other in the fiercest terms is familiar. This may be taken as a sign of their volatility or incorrigible sentimentality; it could also mean that the invisible ties which unite them are ultimately stronger than the physical barriers which divide them. (Mansfield, 1985, p. 469)

THE GOVERNMENT PERSPECTIVE

It is impossible to suggest that one dominant government perspective is apparent in all of the Arab nations, but the predominance of Islam as a religion that has historically viewed religion and state as inseparable aids in some understanding of who makes decisions, upon what criteria, and for what purposes. Tribal autonomy is a deeply felt value, and as a result, many of the Arab nations have had patterns of isolation that have led to divergent rates and paths of development.

In some countries, oil money has facilitated the growth of schools, transportation, and communication infrastructures. In some cases, like Saudi Arabia the new elite constituted by the oil business has at times challenged or contradicted government policy decisions.

Because of the uneven development experienced by Arab nations and the relatively recent wealth experienced by some of those nations, it is possible to see the impact of many recent technological advances as they diffuse throughout traditional cultures. One uniting factor has always been, and will continue to be the Arabic language, which is itself more adapted to oral/aural exchange than to written communication. More than 150 million people from Morocco to the Arabian Sea speak a dialect of Arabic, and can for the most part be understood by other dialect speakers. As a result, the use of audiocassettes and radio has played a huge role in the uniting of Arab nations, and in the political and cultural contexts of each nation. It has been said that the continued importance of readings and renditions of the Holy Koran has helped make classical Arabic more easily understood among the different dialects.

The legacy of colonization left other "official" languages and cultural practices behind, that have also influenced growth and development in and among Arab nations. For example, Libya has been influenced by former Italian colonials, and Morocco, by the French. Still, the traditional unifying factor is that of the dominance of Islam, which enforces its own beliefs on the use of technology and social practices. Similarly, some Arab nations have developed specific development plans, whereas others have emphasized other aspects of the society on which to concentrate. Almost all of the development plans or national budgets for Arab nations include an emphasis on education for the people, reduction of illiteracy, emphasis on health issues, and an increase in electric power. With regard to education, many of the teachers in Arab nations were schooled in Egypt or elsewhere. With regard to power, more eclectic approaches have been taken.

Power is Power

Prior to development and modernization plans of the 1950s sources of power in Arab nations were considered low priority issues. Now, however, electronic technologies require power sources, as do other conveniences, like refrigeration, air conditioning, advanced medical technologies, and so on. Getting electric power to the people has provided some interesting scenarios.

For example, in Egypt, a tax on electricity was placed so that the wealthy, who could afford to have electricity in the home, would absorb the costs and would supplement the costs of electricity for the poor. This approach failed, however, because of the problems the government had in monitoring who had power, was using it, and would pay for it.

In Tehran, a major force of Iranian law and order has been disconnecting illegal and unpaid electricity supplies. According to a recent estimate, a squad of electricians employed for this specific purpose disconnect 500 illegal connections per day (Cragg, 1988).

Still, there are other countries that have been beset by other concerns due to years of drought, internal conflict, and less solvent economies, like the Yemens, United Arab Emirates, and the Sudan. At times, like in Lebanon, the government's plan to develop a power infrastructure was turned over to private developers who then increased cost and accessibility so that few could take advantage of the system.

THE MASSES PERSPECTIVE

As indicated earlier, Islam suggests a class stratification in its own way. In Iran, the upper class includes leaders of Shiite Islam, the ayattollahs, and religious scholars (mujtahids). In urban areas, political leaders and those associated with government occupy the first stratum in the social structure, whereas people from the rural areas are almost always considered a lower class than even the urban poor. Although much emphasis has been concentrated in various literacy campaigns, many of which use the media as a distribution vehicle, the number of illiterates in each nation is a major factor in the use of specific types of technologies for development purposes (see Table 7.1).

The masses perspective then, take into consideration the stratification of each society. Whether the issue is adoption of technologies for development purposes, entertainment, or the notion of raising the standard of one's lifestyle, the technologies, electricity, software, must be made available to a greater number of people throughout the society. In many cases, this may mean that laws and restrictions that keep technologies from the masses (such as import quotas, high tariffs, etc.) must be redefined for greater use by all members of the society, regardless of class or status.

In many of the Arab nations, minority groups are identified by religious and ethnic groups. Additionally, the large-scale construction in the wealthier nations has added a new "lower class" of migrants from the poorer countries who constitute populations of different religious practices and customs, even though their home nations were dominated by Islam as well. Even within some nations (like the Yemens) Islam has taken different forms and has added to tribal factionalism.

Sexual stratification is also endorsed by Islam. Women have greater freedom to travel in either urban or rural areas in some countries, more than in others. For example, in most urban areas, woman may be allowed to work in businesses, or travel about without the traditional shador. In some countries,

TABLE 7.1
Percentage of Illiterates in Population

Country	Year of report	Illiteracy % of population	
Algeria	1971	81.1	
Egypt	1976	61.8	
Liberia	1974	89.0	
Libya	1973	61.0	
Morocco	1971	78.6	
Sudan	1973	68.6	
Yemen (South)	1973	72.9	native
		94.2	nomad
Iran	1976	63.5	
Iraq	1985	10.7	
Jordan	1979	34.6	
Kuwait	1980	32.5	
Lebanon	1970	20.6	
Quatar	1981	48.9	
Saudi Arabia	1982	48.9	
Syria	1970	60	
United Arab Emirates	1975	46.5	

Source: UNESCO (1987).

women may be free to walk unveiled only to certain areas where there are other women, but no men, such as to laundry areas or markets.

These belief-induced practices strongly effect the rate of social technology diffusion. In general, most media policies have intentionally favored men, and have favored the elites; however, the one area in which a greater variety of classes and women have received attention is in the enhancement of education. In South Yemen (the Peoples' Republic of Yemen—the only socialist country in the Arab world), the 1974 family law was passed to change women's status. The law endorsed a minimum age for marriage (16 for women, 18 for men), and attempted to protect the woman's position in divorce. Similarly, the General Union of Yemeni Women (GUYM) attempted to increase women's education and their inclusion in the social production sphere (Nyrop, 1986).

Other concerns of the masses include issues of child labor, particularly in countries where cheap, unskilled labor is required for construction, and the problem of itinerant peoples, such as the beduin.

Telephony

A cursory glance at the varying capacities of telephone systems throughout the Arab nations give a quick reference to the varied rates of development (see Table 7.2).

Although the figures do not indicate where the predominance of telephones exist, it is safe to assume that they are primarily concentrated in

TABLE 7.2
Telephones in the Arab World

Country	Year of report	Telephone receivers
Algeria	1984	709,000
Egypt	—	no report
Iran	1976	800,000
Iraq		
Jordan	1986	177,894
(East Bank only)		
Lebanon		
Libya		
Morocco		
Oman	1984	65,000
Quatar	1986	115,000
Sudan	1983	1,000
Syria	1984	582,000

Source: Compiled from reports in *The Middle East and North Africa, 35th edition*, London, Europa Publications, Ltd. 1988.

urban areas. In many cases, such as in Saudi Arabia, the extremely wealthy shahs in rural areas have also had telephone service in the form of dedicated wires to the nearest switching system, which might be many, many miles away.

Almost all of the Arab nations that do have development plans have included the enhancement of the telecommunications systems as a target area. Iran has traditionally had the most sophisticated and far-reaching telephone system in the Middle East (Nyrop, 1978) but the system had been purchased through agreement with AT&T of the United States. When the U.S. government ceased activity with Iran, the continued development of the telephone system was stopped. Another company could not expand on the AT&T system for contractual and technological compatibility reasons, and the Iranian phone system has remained incomplete (Mowlana, 1987).

Saudi Arabia has included plans to increase the telephone system by 250,000 subscribers in its fifth national development plan, 1985/1986–1990/ 1991 (*Handbook of National Development Plans,* Vol. 1, 1988), making it the fastest growing Arab nation in telephone development and use.

The Impact of Radio and Television

Arabic has emerged to become a dominant broadcast language for external radio services throughout the world (see Table 7.3). Boyd (1982) has written extensively on telecommunication systems in the Arab nations, and has indicated how great a role both domestic and international radio has played over the years. What emerges then, is a culture that seems to have easily adapted to the innovation of the radio medium, but that still registers a greater level of concern for the more visually oriented media. Furthermore, the use of radio not only as a tool for unification, but also as a means of propaganda, makes it a dominant medium for all of the Arab nations, and therefore has traditionally been geared to a more male audience. Particularly since the escalation of the Middle East wars, other nations have increased the amount of external radio in Arabic to the area (see Table 7.3).

In the areas of radio and television, Egypt has undoubtedly held the lead ahead of other Arab nations. This is in large part due to the efforts of Gamal Abdel Nasser, President of Egypt from 1954–1970. According to Boyd (1977):

> Probably better than any other Middle Eastern leader, he understood the uses to which the mass media, particularly broadcasting, could be put for political advantage. While Nasser's role in Middle East and specifically Egyptian history is both applauded and scorned, he is remembered as a man who tried to bring Egypt and the rest of the Arab Middle East a measure of strength and unity. (pp. 2–3)

TABLE 7.3
External Radio Focused on Arab Nations

Europe

BBC—England   70 hrs/wk.—During 7 Day War, escalated to 120 hrs/wk.
Deutsche Welle—West Germany   32 hrs/wk.
Radio Exterior de Espana—Spain   31 hrs/wk.
Radio Nederland—Holland   22 hrs/wk.
RAI—Italy   14 hrs/wk.
SRI—Swiss Radio International   3½ hrs/wk.
Greece—4 hrs/wk.

Soviet Countries

Radio Moscow—U.S.S.R.   49 hrs/wk.
Radio Peace and Progress—U.S.S.R.   ½ hr/day (also called "Voice of Soviet Public
   Opinion")
East Germany—49 hrs/wk.
Bulgaria—21 hrs/wk.
Albania—21 hrs/wk (when Albania and the Peoples' Republic of China were closer,
Albania radio relayed some of China's Arabic service)
Poland—17½ hrs/wk.
Czechoslovakia   14 hrs/wk.
Romania—14 hrs/wk.
Yugoslavia hrs/wk.—7 hrs/wk.
North Korea—42 hrs/wk.
Peoples' Republic of China—14 hrs/wk.
Afghanistan—3½ hrs/wk.

Asia and the Middle East

AIR—India 17½ hrs/wk—first country to broadcast in Arabic (1941)
Pakistan—28 hrs/wk.
Iran—10½ hrs/wk.
Bangladesh—3½ hrs/wk.
Indonesia—7 hrs/wk.
Sri Lanka—5 min/day.
Turkey—1 hr/wk.
Malaysia—10½ hrs/wk.
Japan—3½ hrs/wk.
South Korea—1½ hr/day.
Taiwan—14 hrs/wk.

The Americas

Voice of America (VOA)—U.S.   7½ hrs/day.
Radio Habana Cuba—2 hrs/day.
Chile—14 hrs/day.
Venezuela—7 hrs/day.

Sub-Saharan Africa

Nigeria—10½ hrs/wk.
Somalia—7 hrs/wk.
Senegal—1¾ hrs/wk.
*Radio Voice of the Gospel—Ethiopia—1 hr/day.

Christian Religious Broadcasting

Trans World Radio (New Jersey) owns and leases studios and transmitters around the world; many of these broadcasters take advantage of the TWR facilities.

TWR—8¼ hrs/wk.
ELWA (Eternal Love Winning Africa) from Liberia—13½ hrs/wk.
Far East Broadcasting Assn.   2 hrs/day
Radio Vaticana   3½ hrs/wk.
WYFR—Family Stations, Oakland, California   3½ hrs/wk.

Source: Boyd (1982).
*Radio Voice of the Gospel operated by the Lutheran Church until the Ethiopian government nationalized the service.

Voice of the Arabs. As a unifying factor, a radio network was constructed to aid in Arab nationalism. Begun on July 4, 1953, one year after the Egyptian Revolution *Voice of the Arabs* premiered. The idea for the original program came from Abdel-Kader Hatem who served Egypt in several information posts including Minister of Information, although it is believed Nasser wrote most of the content.

The radio service began as a 30-minute a day broadcast and quickly grew to a 24-hour service broadcast on short and medium wave. It was not the only source of information in the Middle East programmed by Arabs, and often it became confused with Radio Cairo, the main Egyptian service for Egyptians.

For the first 3 years the Voice concentrated on various political struggles in the Maghreb. As a propaganda tool, the service was used to support the cause of French-exiled Sultan Mohammed V in Morocco as well as for Habib Bourguiba's neo-Destrou party in Tunisia. It gave support to the Algerian revolution and allowed its facilities to be used by Algerian revolutionary leaders who were based in Cairo.

Although it generally maintained a broad appeal, it targeted certain regions during certain parts of the day. Programs were designed for the Gulf states, Lebanon and Syria, and the southern peninsula with programming that often consisted of news and commentary, press reviews from Egyptian papers, speeches, talks by and interviews with various Arab politicians, and dramas with political themes and music.

After 3 years, it began to support Nasser's Middle East political aspirations and by the mid-1950s it established itself as an enthusiastic medium for revolutionary propaganda. Under Nasser, Egypt adopted an anti-colonialist, anti-imperialist position, and although anti-Zionist themes were ever present, the attention was toward various Arab countries. Egypt and Syria united into the United Arab Republic in 1958 and extended the use of transmitters for the Voice. British and U.S. sources tried to stop broadcasts that were hostile to the West, but Nasser replied:

How can I reach my power base? My power lies with the Arab masses. The only way I can reach my people is by radio. If you ask me for radio disarmament, it means that you are asking me for complete disarmament. (Heikal, 1973, cited in Boyd, 1977, p. 28)

The Voice finally began to lose power as more radio came into the area from other nations and locations. Additionally, the listeners began to understand that name-calling strategies and bias might not be entirely true, and eventually, the Voice moderated its tone. The Voice lost credibility in the Middle East War of 1967 when announcers kept telling the people that Egypt was winning the war, but the message was contradicted by other radio stations.

Television.   The largest production house for Arab television is in Cairo. Egypt already had a film industry that provided content for the distribution medium, which easily led the way for Egypt to dominate the world in Arab production. From the 1950s Egypt has sought technical, equipment, and other types of aid from countries, but although Nasser was more inclined to deal with Russia, the TV technology and facilities in the West were better and became the technical standard.

For a time during and after the Middle East War, other Arab nations rejected Egypt's control over televised content because of Egypt's siding with Israel. Many other countries—all except Oman and Sudan (angry with Egypt for negotiating peace with Israel) attempted to produce their own product, and new production companies were established in Jordan, Tunisia, Dubai, and Abu Dhabi; also Greece, West Germany, and Britain. Now, even Libya and Syria are buying again.

The content of Egyptian TV is, however, primarily Egyptian. Many dramas have religious or patriotic themes. Islamic beliefs lead censors and producers not to violate codes of modest dress or focus on political themes that might offend one regime or another. Islamic practices limit content of much of the entertainment programming that comes to Arab countries. For example, a U.S. program shown in Saudi Arabia might have parts edited that show "too much" of a woman's body, or "suggestive" physical acts. Pornography is strictly forbidden, with punishment for the smuggling of potentially pornographic materials a major offense. Pornography includes any material that might conflict with the tenets and beliefs of Islam.

A criticism of Egyptian TV is that it will do nothing to alienate its biggest markets, Saudi Arabia and the Gulf, which are the most conservative areas. Another criticism that is shared by many indigenous productions is that Arab television is too slow. Slick U.S. or European content is far more appealing and thus, the videocassette market has grown tremendously (see Table 7.4).

TABLE 7.4
Arab Nations: Radio–TV Availability

	per 1,000			
	Radio Receivers		TV Receivers	
Country	1975	1985	1975	1985
Algeria	187	221	31	72
Egypt	141	256	17	82
Liberia	167	228	5.7	16
Libya	206	222	35	65
Morrocco	81	175	26	52
Sudan	72	251	6.2	51
Yemen (South)	58	70	18	19
Yemen (North)	16	22	—	4.1
Iran	61	224	51	56
Iraq	114	189	37	57
Jordan	173	225	46	68
Kuwait	—	274	—	235
Lebanon	477	787	148	300
Quatar	—	—	117	381
Saudi Arabia	131	321	—	269
Syria	—	238	30	57
United Arab Emirates	103	264	50	98

Source: Compiled from UNESCO Statistical Yearbook (1987).
Radio and Television reports reflect times (—) when no data was available.

Although many of the countries in the region have their own television systems (most of which are state controlled), the ARABVISION system encourages daily exchanges of television programs and information among the various countries.

Audiocassettes.   According to Ganley and Ganley (1987) the most systematic and successful use of audiocassettes for political purposes has been in Iran, where, under the Ayatollah Khomeini, cassettes were used to distribute copies of the Ayattolah's direct-dialed telephone conversations to Iran while he was in exile in Iraq (from 1965 to October 1987) and Paris (October 1978 to the end of January 1979). Before his death, the Ayatollah used both audio and videocassettes to spread his message to the people of Iran, and for propaganda purposes to Egypt and Turkey.

During the 1970s, an "underground" culture of audiocassette distribution began to form, emanating from Egypt and Lebanon, with content including poetry, religion, politics, economics, philosophy, songs, and news and political analysis (Khalifallah, 1983). The underground cassettes have spawned stars, some of whom are considered politically "incorrect" by various government standards. For example, Egyptian lutist Sheikh Imam's cassettes may bring as much as 10 years of imprisonment to anyone found in possession of them in Jordan, Saudi Arabia, Oman or Bahrain.

Although Egypt is the central clearinghouse and censorship board for Arab videocassettes (see Table 7.5), it also makes a considerable amount of money by licensing them. The VCR has enabled people in nations without theaters to see dramatic productions from other Arab nations as well as imports from the West, and because they are viewed in the home, both men and women may view together, changing the tradition of segregated entertainment outside of the home.

Both audio- and videocassettes are also popular vehicles for Middle Eastern plays that usually have political themes, and the popularity of cassettes has given impetus to many bootleg copies, some of which are several generations down from the original tape.

Because of the censorship and illegal activity in tape duplication, some governments have taken a hard line on "inappropriate" or black-market materials. In Iran, U.S. videocassettes are very popular, as are rock and pornographic videotapes, but penalties for inappropriate cassettes there, are more severe than any Arab country. Penalties for unapproved videocassettes may range from 2 to 12 months of jail, to a death sentence (Ganley & Ganley, 1987, citing USIA unclassified cable, 1985). In Saudi Arabia, foreign-

TABLE 7.5
VCR and Television Penetration in the Arab Nations

Country	TV sets in use	VCRs
Arab Republic of Egypt	3,850,000	1.05
Iran	2,000,000	.36
Iraq	500,000	9.76
Libyan Arab Republic	235,000	80.31
Peoples Democratic Republic of Yemen	30,000	.00
Qatar	100,000	68.44
Saudi Arabia	1,500,000	50.76
United Arab Emirates	1,000,000	505.16
Yemen Arab Republic	n/a	.00
the Sudan	90,000	.20
Lebanon	600,000	12.26
Syria		
Jordan	200,000	14.29
Bharain	120,000	51.29
Oman	40,000	124.99
Algeria	1,140,000	.12
Morrocco	687,700	.15
Tunisia	385,000	.00

Source: UNESCO (1987).

ers bringing in any cassette that is considered to be pornographic may also be incarcerated or deported.

Where people buy videocassette players is another issue; wealthy Arabs can bring them into the country with little problem, but they then sometimes sell their extra VCRs to the less wealthy. This also makes VCRs popular in the stolen goods markets.

Regional Cooperation for Technical Use

For telematic media, many Arab nations have cooperated for the production of media content and for greater access to the most expensive infrastructures. The Arab States Broadcasting Union (ASBU) has effectively promoted news exchanges and cooperative audience research, training, and technical efforts; and have cooperated with the European Broadcast Union (EBU) to conduct a daily satellite relay for North American and European television distribution.

In the area of satellites, the Arab nations have sponsored ARABSAT to augment the limited availability of INTELSAT transponders available to Arab nations for television, telephone, and computer data transfer. Headquartered in Riyadh, Saudi Arabia, ARABSAT has been implemented with the aid of France, and now has three satellites; ARABSAT 1 (launched in February 1985), ARABSAT 2 (launched in June 1985), and ARABSAT 3 (ready to be launched if either ARABSAT 1 or 2 break down).

The ARABSAT transponders have enabled communications to span several time zones, and it is possible to broadcast television for 16 hours a day.

In addition to television, the satellites provide additional telephone circuits and mobile services to underdeveloped regions. Plans have been constructed to use ARABSAT information for emergency services, disaster relief management, and to bring medical information to remote sites.

For both the ASBU and ARABSAT, the wealthier Arab nations have contributed funds with the poorer Arab nations paying a smaller percentage, or receiving less use of the services. Recently, however, some of the wealthier nations have begun to question the soundness of this contributory scheme, and may at some date choose to end this type of arrangement.

The Cultural Contexts

Several nations have been mentioned in previous sections with regard to specific technologies or social practices. The following thumbnail sketches provide a little greater insight into some of the individual nations' plans for technological adoption and social acceptance. Only those nations with unique perspectives have been chosen for attention. Almost all of the nations have had specific development plans, but the success of those plans generally rests on how wealthy the nation has become.

Egypt. As indicated by Egypt's efforts to develop film, television, and radio industries, the country has a long history of development plans. The first national development plan took place in 1960/1961–1964/1965, and have continued along the 5-year plan style since then, with the greatest amount of growth from 1973 to 1981/1982 (*Handbook of National Development Plans,* 1988). With a relatively stable electricity infrastructure, Egypt has made greater use of the broadcast media and has begun to use mainframe and minicomputers on a greater scale than any other Arab nation.

Part of Egypt's success in infrastructure and development planning, has been the attention to education as a critical component of development. Throughout the Arab world, the greatest number of Arab-trained teachers in schools come from Egypt, the nation with the most sophisticated school and university system.

Saudi Arabia. The wealthiest of the Arab nations, but one of the most conservative, Saudi Arabia has adopted media technologies faster than social technologies. Boyd and Straubhaar (1985) have written that Saudi Arabia:

> decided to go into television in the mid-60s because Islamic leaders believed that it would be an ideal medium in the Islamic family-oriented society and that the government would be the cultural, as well as the entertainment and information gatekeeper . . . (p. 11)

Conservatives in Saudi Arabia voiced opposition to television in the early days, stating that it was "blasphemous," and "potentially corrupting . . . as another western element" (Boyd, 1982, p. 129). Throughout the years there have been several public actions by different interest groups supporting or refuting television, but the tight censorship of Saudi television has quelled some of the initial outcry.

Saudi Arabia has also met most of the development goals outlined by official development plans, and has completed major infrastructural plans, at least for now. One problem in meeting these goals is that the needs determined by government planners in the past may have been adequate for the past; as other parts of society develop, those former goals need to be reassessed. For example, the town of Abha was allocated sufficient telephone lines and switching systems for the size of the town, but when a major U.S. firm decided to build a conference center and hotel on the town's outskirts all of the allocated telephone facilities were commandeered by the hotel, and the people of the town have yet to be able to get telephone service.

The importance is Islam is most obvious in Saudi society. The primary goal of the current national development plan, 1985/1986 – 1990/1991 specifically states that the goal of development is to "safeguard Islamic values" (*Handbook of National Development Plans*, 1988, p. 10, Saudi Arabia). Although technological changes are made in the society they primarily benefit the elite, as unemployment of the lower classes is still a major problem.

The Sudan.   The Sudan has attempted to implement development plans, and has had three 5-year development plans, all of which have been severely effected by the three seasons of poor rainfall, recession, famine, and poor export market. The primary development goal for 1985–2000 is the national energy plan that will have a priority list of electricity users that will benefit the elite, but will also serve to attract the attention of foreign investment.

North Yemen.   North Yemen is not as developed as South Yemen, and has significantly more problems with making health care available to all of its people. Additionally, the tremendous migration of Yemeni people to labor in the construction trades in Saudi Arabia has witnessed a drain of public resources in the country.

The two Yemens have stated a desire to eventually unify, but the North is more politically committed to the monarchy in Saudi Arabia (although it received military training from the Soviet Union), whereas the South is more economically and ideologically tied to the Soviet Union.

South Yemen.   The Peoples' Democratic Republic of Yemen (PDRY) has had a series of national development plans, starting in 1971. Between 1981 and 1985, telecommunications and transport were the fastest growing areas (14.5% of the development budget) (*Handbook of National Development Plans*, Vol. 2, 1988). The government has attempted to raise private capital to finance further development.

The PDRY has had remarkable success in improving literacy and raising the educational standards for children and women. Between 1966 and 1981 a total of 700 new schools were built; the military also ran boarding school for beduin children to integrate the tribal children into the national culture (Nyrop, 1986).

Iran.   Iran uses television, audio, and videocassettes for religious purposes, causing it to be called "mullah-vision," or "the wooley glass" because of the number of bearded mullahs it features (Hanley, 1982). Also tightly controlled by the government, the media support Islamic values through content and structure. As a result, many of the cassettes have also been used as disinformation and propaganda tools, such as that used to support the deposing of the Shah, by the Ayattolahs. As indicated earlier in this chapter, sources of electric power exist, but primarily in and for the urban dwellers.

Iraq. Iraq was the first Arab nation to establish a media system that was operated by the government. The content of the media is primarily political (and religious), and the dominant philosophy since the 1958 revolution has been to downplay the ideas of the West.

Kuwait. Although a small nation, Kuwait is a wealthy one, with a good number of the people well educated. It is one of the few Arab nations that actively invests in projects outside the country, and has a philosophy of broadcasting in both Arabic and English to its people.

Libya. Broadcasting in Libya, like most Arab nations, is a function of the state, run by the People's Revolutionary Broadcasting Co., (PRBC). Libya's program for development takes into consideration the strong legacy left by Italian and Greek colonizers, and the effects they have left on the culture.

When Libya gained independence in 1951, education was a major problem; 14 people in the country had college degrees out of a population of 3 million, although the literacy rate was at 81%. Since the discovery of oil, many rural dwellers have flocked to the cities, calling for development priorities that address housing, health, and food. The media have been used as tools of mobilization and motivation throughout the revolution, but the government has not developed media as a priority.

Radio is the dominant medium because of its affordability and portability, and has served as the primary source of information and news throughout the various crises in recent Libyan history. Laborers make use of radio as they work, thereby emphasizing the social component of the audience; television requires leisure time and is a very expensive medium, compared to radio, and thus, less emphasis has been given to development of TV and other video technologies. Interestingly, however, Libyan television does have limited broadcasting in both French and English, for the approximately 15% of the Libyan population that reside in the country (McDaniel, 1982).

THE ARAB NATIONS AND THE INFORMATION SOCIETY

In the development of the Arab information society (see Fig. 7.1), economic, cultural, and technological contexts play equally important roles. The oil revenues have expedited the aspirations for technology expansion through mainly the importing of technology, importing of technical human resources, and the levels of indigenous production of technologies remain low.

National Policies ◄──────► Resources ◄──────► Inputs ◄──────► Output

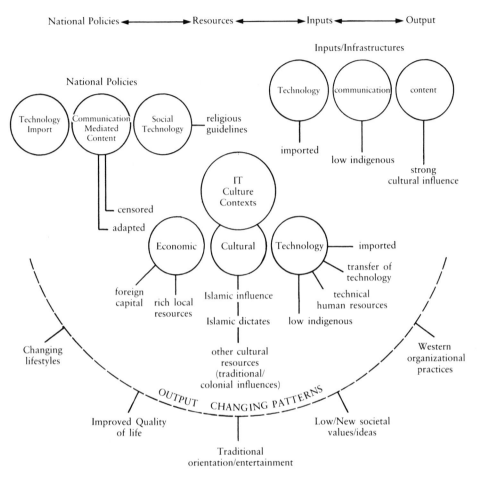

FIG. 7.1.   Information society model: Arab countries.

The social technology perspective of these communication technologies is dominated by the cultural context that holds religion above other influences. Because of the relationship of the religion to other factors, all social practices reflect the practices of Islam.

THE INFORMATION TECHNOLOGY MODEL

The information technology model in Arab nations focuses on gaining technological power through increased economic gains brought about by oil money (see Fig. 7.2). Both foreign capital as well as local economic resources are utilized for diffusion of information, innovations, and social change. The communication technologies are used for political and religious purposes to support dominant beliefs. Even though advanced technologies may be considered for structural facilitation of activities, the purposes remain rooted in traditional practices and beliefs.

The diffusion of information power is located at the elite levels, primarily within the powerful family control of governments, but there are still efforts at regional cooperation among the Arab nations for a sharing of information power.

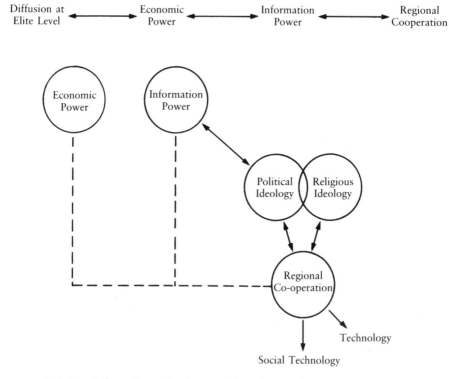

FIG. 7.2. Information technology model: Arab countries.

SUMMARY

Technologies are causing change at rapid rates in some Arab nations. Traditional social practices are changing due to technological innovation but for the most part the changes reflect sweeping social and cultural changes brought about by tremendous amounts of money in the oil-rich nations. Those changes are creating stress for the Islamic ideals held by many of the dominant governments.

Political exigencies have caused major concerns for national and regional development, and the importance of Islam has dictated how and in what way social technologies are practiced. The "less wealthy" nations are benefiting somewhat from regional organizations, but are experiencing change at a slower rate, and are also subject to the vicissitudes of the more powerful countries.

Certainly what is apparent in the Arab nations is the amount of control of those who have the financial resources and the social status within society. If predictions are correct that Islamic fundamentalism will become a dominant world force in the next few years, the relationship of social technologies and technical innovations may be more uniform and complementary.

The Arab nations and Iran provide a sense of what can be done in development when financial resources are not a problem; but they also clearly exemplify the position that social technologies are needed for integration and adaptation within a society.

Conclusions and Recommendations

A policy has to include some degree of conscious determination about future action.

—Ove Granstrand (1981)

Historically, communication technologies have been perceived alternatively as salvation and threat; and although they are most decidedly not neutral artifacts, they should be considered for what they are—means of communication that relate to existing social structures within societies. Technologies and policies that affect innovation and use are specifically agents of change that can seldom be reversed. There are, however, levels at which the control of technologies and software can be perceived as both beneficial and pro-social. Policies that are created to serve these needs are the most likely to gain acceptance by a wider range of individuals within the social structure.

DIFFERENCE IN INFORMATION SOCIETY NEEDS, DEMANDS, AND MODELS

Information resources, national policies, and needs and demands for information technology interact to create specific information environments, culture, and models. These are very specific to each country, as evidenced by the case studies presented in this volume. Some of the countries included here focus on diffusion of information technology at the grassroots level, others at the elite level. Some want to use information technology for social transformation, others for political power. Depending on what the objective or goal is, they have different ways to deal with this information problem.

Applications of Policy Decisions

Policy decisions for technology are affected by various factors such as political, economic, cultural, and technological factors. Our studies show that political factors are the most important for the acceptance of technology. Without political support (for domestic or external sources of technology) innovation is impossible.

Cultural factors are the next in importance for technology acceptance and use. Like the cultural contexts, cultural ideology, and the cultural challenges, cultural factors make technology work within any system. Tradition is one of the most important concepts for a developing nation to work within, and therefore the importance of tradition and culture set parameters in which to identify appropriate needs and channels for acceptance of change by and through technology.

The availability of economic resources is important for establishing, maintaining, developing, and diffusing technologies for practical use. Although we have ranked economic resources as the third priority, they of course must reflect the dominant cultural and political ideologies and practices.

Technology itself is important, but without the first three factors it would be impossible to situate the technology in its proper context. Along with technological hardware we must include software, which suggests a sometimes very important lowcost alternative to cultural domination and the enhancement of using technology within a cultural context.

The Social Technology Perspective

The discussions in this book show that the government, the people, and the media community are all equally important actors in the diffusion of innovations for information technology and ultimate development of the information society. Equally important, however, is how these three actions accept the cultural challenges of different technologies at different points in time.

Our studies also show that theoretical conceptions of culture lag, the innovation process, technological determinism and liberalism, and the organization of international groups have important interpretive consequences for adequate understanding of the cultural context and cultural challenges.

Information Power and the Information Society

Why and how is information power and the information society different than what has been the operating normative constraints within these nations? Different stages of social and political development and technology acceptance may be part of the reason and the cause. We look for solutions to these problems by focusing on the information society and technology models because that is the entry point for a conceptualization of the cultural context, and because it is at this entry point where we may best assess the philosophies and pragmatics involved in establishing and maintaining communications infrastructures within nations.

As evidenced by many of the studies in this book, practices are often different from policies; sometimes accidentally, but more often because of confrontation within government controls that are antithetical to other social dimensions such as needs or desires.

The structures imposed by technological systems have seldom been questioned for their social impact by developing nations. For example, centralized, pyramidal hierarchical systems and supersystems necessitated for telecommunications and informatics may indeed assure presence on an international playing field, when attention to domestic use of decentralized group and network technologies may well do more to enhance development. Certainly the decisions to develop some aspects of information technology to the exclusion or suppression of others is a difficult task, but crucial to determining the future of a nation in the information society.

Power, as it is perceived by government officials and elites often overrides decisions when massive expenditures or precious resources are at stake. So many concepts of power have been linked to international exchange of information and establishing a strong national presence, that attention to smaller forms of media (such as ethnotronics) have often been ignored when they could well assure an acceptance of technology at a level more likely conducive to change with a more prosocial benefit.

RECOMMENDATIONS

We have been discussing the multifaceted approaches to the use of technology within developing nations. The major focus reflects cost access (appropriate technology), cost effectiveness, and possession of technology.

Recommendation 1: Cost Access

The key to more information flow is *cost access*. We identify cost access with buying power to have more and more actual ownership of hardware and software systems, which will be possible if these technologies are cost effective. If more people have access to ownership, the diffusion escalates and technologies may be made even more cost effective. The salient point is that the cost factors should be relevant to the specific country's financial capability/buying power. A cost of a $20 technology in one country may be acceptable in another country at $300. If the nation cannot support even lower costs, nothing can be done.

In seeking appropriate technologies, the cultural context could determine types of social/technological practices. The Alphonsin administration of Argentina provided an example of bringing social groups together to work with and in response to the limited database available through government channels in the CONICET project. Likewise, use of radio as a low-cost means to educational enhancement in many countries, particularly in the ASEAN and Pacific Rim, is a good example of what can be done within the parameters of limited financial resources. Other possibilities afforded by information technologies include electronic computer networking on the domestic and international levels, and desktop publishing for the production of low-cost materials through the use of microcomputers.

Granted, these considerations are far more practical in developing nations that have reasonably efficient sources of electric power, but the decentralization measures inherent in these technologies circumvent some of the most difficult problems, such as the vast rural communities and inequalities in literacy. Technological uses on the local scale are more adaptable to indigenous materials and less likely to fall victim to prepackaged, culturally dominated software, as evidenced by videocassettes.

Recommendation 2: Cost Effectiveness

This element requires government policies that are responsive to big and small media; infrastructural support and ethnotronic technologies. In many countries governments have exercised what they believe is control by creating policies that impede the use of new technologies, but the the potential for change is less in the technology itself than in the use of the system or by means of software. Exorbitant taxes and duties on imported equipment may foster illicit activity, whereas at the same time integration and attention to lower cost software development might be a counter measure to black-market trade in materials that may be perceived (on the government level) to threaten cultural values.

Personal use, family, and community decisions also effect the ownership and use patterns to be supported by a specific society, as do resources such as electric power, indigenous manufacture, and government policies such as import quotas and movement of goods "informally," through migration patterns. The trend toward privatization sacrifices the power of both the government and the social groups to respond directly to matters of effective social use of the media and introduces concepts that impede cost effectiveness.

Accepting technology in social environments such as schools, social groups, or other various organizations may enhance cost effectiveness if attention can be turned to the experimentation and creation of software that reflects local interests and values. One unique quality of much of today's information technology is the very personal nature of its use that reflects a relationship between machine and human that can enhance tradition, religious beliefs, or other such interests—depending on the context of use.

Recommendation 3: Possession of Technology

The studies in this book have shown that the cultural context and cultural ideology are very important for the development and acceptance of a particular technology as well as for the enhancement of a specific technological system. The acceptance within the cultural context and the ideological context pose cultural challenges for policymakers to be responsive to the needs of all people within a society; therefore, the possession of technology must be regarded not as alien, but as an enhancement to practices.

Rapidly shifting political allegiances and economic debt is a reality for many developing nations, particularly in Latin America; Islamic fundamentalism in the Arab nations is likewise, as important a distinct expression of cultural context that poses a special challenge. Inequities in social practices among regions that share cultures in the ASEAN and Pacific Rim nations also display a unique set of characteristics for development considerations. But the important factor is that in each nation and group of nations, the cultural challenges that are now prevalent, may also be subject to change in the future. Projections for the future cannot deny the past or the present, and policies must be developed that can change as well.

THE SOCIAL TECHNOLOGY PERSPECTIVE:
CONFIGURATIONS TO CHANGE

The social technology perspective to information flow emphasizes the value configurations such as work ethics and organizational practices, regard for human nature, relationships of people to nature, time orientations, orientations toward activity, and the types of relations among people. These have been discussed in the context of country and regional case studies presented in this book, and it is apparent that the emphasis on these values differs from country to country. Within the cultural contexts these value configurations must be developed to match the technological innovations. This needs the concerted effort of all three actors: government, masses, and the media community. The value configuration creates an information environment and an appropriate mental set to accept and influence the information environment.

The information society then, is not a utopian society; nor is it a global village, or a capitalist convention in which information is a commodity that is bought and sold. The real information society represents and celebrates diversity within cultural contexts. It acknowledges that power influences dynamics within and among nations, but it fosters communication and a *relationship of interaction among peoples of a nation, and among nations of the world.* Thus, the traditional notion of power as something that controls actions is relegated to a place as an interpretive tool and the importance of the individual in society—the worth of the human being—is elevated to the pre-eminent concern for the rights of individuals within their societies. Information is a tool for change, and technologies a means to create change. The cultural challenges involve a determination of what change can, will, and must take place.

References

Abundo, R. B. (1985). *Print and broadcast media in the south pacific* Singapore: AMIC.

Adler, E. (1987). *The power of ideology: The quest for technological autonomy in Argentina and Brazil.* Berkeley, CA: University of California Press.

Akhtar, R. (1985). *Pakistan yearbook, 13th edition 1985–1986.* Karachi-Lahore: East and West Publishing.

Albornoz, M. (1987, September). *Aportes Para la Formulacion de la Politica Científica Y Technologica en Argentina.* [Contributions to the formulation of a scientific and technological policy in Argentina]. Paper presented to the conference on Prospectiva Para la Formulacion De Politicas Y Estrategias En Ciencia y Technologia [Prospects for the formulation of policies and strategies in science and technology], Buenos Aires.

Alisky, M. (1981). *Latin American media: Guidance and censorship.* Ames, IA: Iowa State University Press.

Althusser, L. (1971). Ideology and ideological state apparatuses. In B. Brewster (Trans.), *Lenin and philosophy, and other essays* (pp. 127–186) New York: New Left Books.

Asia Computer Weekly. (1989, June).

Basu, A. (1987). Grass roots movements and the state *Theory and Society* 16(5), 647–674.

Buch, T. (1987, September). *Perspectivas De La Prospectiva* [Perspectives and prospects]. Paper presented at the conference on Prospectiva Para la Formulacion De Politicas Y Estrategias En Ciencia Y Technologia [Prospects for the formulation of policies and strategies in science and technology], Buenos Aires.

Bernard, J. (1987). *The female world from a global perspective.* Bloomington, IN: Indiana University Press.

Bell, D. (1973). *The coming of the post-industrial society.* New York: Basic Books.

Boyd, D. A. (1982). *Broadcasting in the Arab world.* Philadelphia, PA: Temple University Press.

Boyd, D. A. (1977). Egyptian radio: Tool of political and national development. *Journalism Monographs, 48.*

Boyd, D. A., & Straubhaar, J. (1985). Developmental impact of the home video cassette recorder on third world countries. *Journal of Broadcasting & Electronic Media,* 29(1), 5–21.

Brennan, M. (1987). *A content analysis of Argentina's television programming, 1976–1983.* Unpublished honors thesis, University of Massachusetts at Amherst, Amherst, MA.

Bunge, F. M. (Ed.). (1983a). *Burma: A country study.* Washington, DC: U.S. Government Printing Office.

Bunge, F. M. (Ed.). (1983b). *Indonesia: A country study.* Washington, DC: U.S. Government Printing Office.

Bunge, F. M. (Ed.). (1984). *Malaysia: Country studies* (4th ed.). Washington, DC: U.S. Government Printing Office.

Bunge, F. M. (Ed.). (1981). *Thailand: A country study.* Washington, DC: U.S. Government Printing Office.

Cardoso, F. H., & Faletto, E. (1979). *Dependency and development in Latin America* Berkeley, Los Angeles, & London: University of California Press.

Clarke, A. C. (1981). New communication technologies and the developing world. *Media Asia, 8*(4), 185–190.

Codding, G. A., Jr. (1979). The new nations and the international telecommunication union: Some policy implications for the future. In H. S. Dordick (Ed.), *Proceedings of the sixth annual telecommunications policy research conference* (pp. 357–360). Lexington, MA: Lexington Books/D.C. Heath.

Cragg, C. (1988). Electricity in the Middle East and North Africa. In *The Middle East and North Africa.* (35th ed., pp. 177–181). London: Europa Publication Ltd.

Cuanto Cuesta la TV Oficial [How much official TV costs]. (1987). *Somos, 10,* 38–42.

Curras, E. (1987). Intelligence and communication within the system theory. In E. V. Smith, S. Keenan, & P. D. Strochan (Eds.), *Information, communications and technology transfer* (pp. 65–74), North Holland: Elsevier.

Davey, G. J. (1988, August). Dynamic changes in southeast asian telecommunication services: Emerging opportunities and regional solutions. *Asia Week,* 8–10.

Department of Telecommunications. (1987). *Telecom Mission draft report.* New Delhi: India.

Dervin, B. (1986). More will be less. *Communicator, 21* 44–46.

Deutsche, K. (1963). Some problems in the study of nation-building. In K. W. Deutsch & W. J. Foltz (Eds.), *Nation-building* (pp. 1-16). New York: Prentice-Hall.

Dexter, G. L. (1987, August). Tuning in on tango land. *Popular Communications,* 10–13.

Diaz-Bordenave, J. (1976). Communication of agricultural innovations. In E. Rogers (Ed.), *Communication and development: Critical perspectives* (pp. 43–62). Beverly Hills, CA: Sage.

Ellul, J. (1985). Preconceived ideas about mediated information. In E. M. Rogers & F. Balle (Eds.), *The media revolution in America and Western Europe* (pp. 95–107). Norwood, NJ: Ablex.

ESCAP Executive Secretary. (1986, November). Address to the Asia Pacific Center for Transfer of Technology, New Delhi, India.

Far East and Australasia, 1988, 19th Ed., (1987). London: Europa Publications.

Ferguson, M. (1986). Industrial, cultural and social strategies. In M. Ferguson (Ed.), *New communication technologies and the public interest* (p. 52). Beverly Hills, CA: Sage.

Foucault, M. (1979). *Discipline and punish: The birth of the prison.* New York: Vintage.

Friere, P. (1985). *Pedagogy of the oppressed.* New York: Continuum.

Frischtak, C. (1986). Brazil. In F. W. Rushing & C. G. Brown (Eds.), *National policies for developing high technology industries, international comparisons* (pp. 32–48). Boulder, CO: Westview Special Studies.

Gandhi, R. (1986, November). Address to the Asia Pacific Center for Transfer of Technology, New Delhi, India.

Ganley, G. D., & Ganley, O. H. (1987) *Goblal political fallout: The first decade of the VCR 1976–1985.* Cambridge, MA: Harvard Program on Information Resources Policy.

Gauhar, A. (1984). Interview with Raul Alfonsin. *South, 48,* 24–25.

Graham-Yooll, A. (1985). Argentina: The state of transition, 1983–1985 *Third World Quarterly, 7,* 573–593.

Granstrand, O. (1981). Some basic concepts and models. In O. Granstrand & J. Sigurdson (Eds.), *Technological and industrial policy in China and Europe: Proceedings from the first joint TIPCE conference, 1981* (pp. 8–15). Lund, Sweden: Research Policy Institute.

Halloran, J. D. (1986). The social implications of technological innovations. In M. Traber (Ed.), *The myth of the information revolution* (pp. 46–63). London: Sage.

Hamelink, C. J. (1983). *Cultural autonomy in global communications.* New York: Longman.

Handbook of national development plans (Vol. 1&2). (1988). London: Graham & Trotman.

Hanley, C. J. (1982). Today's focus: In the age of Khomeini, Tehran moves at half-step. *Nexis.*

Hanson, J. (1987). New principles for the information age. In I. B. Singh & V. M. Mishra (Eds.), *Dynamics of information management* (pp. 50–58). Norwood, NJ: Ablex.

Hills, J. (1986). *Deregulating telecoms.* Westport, CT: Quorum Books.

Howell, W. J., Jr. (1984). *Broadcasting in the age of the satellite.* Norwood, NJ: Ablex.

Information Malaysia 1987 yearbook. (1987). Kuala Lumpur, Malaysia: Berita Publishers.

Information technologies and development. (1986, June). In *ATAS Bulletin* (Vol. 3). New York: United Nations.

Investing in Brazil. (1987, March 31). *The New York Times,* p. A3.

Jabbar, J. (1983). Pakistan: A cautious welcome. *InterMedia, II,* 65–66.

Joshi, P. C. (1988). Inaugural address. *The Communicator, 23,*(1–2), 3.

Jussawalla, M. (in press). Research constraints in the field for communication economics. In U. Narula & W. B. Pearce (Eds.), *Cultures, politics and research programs: An international assessment of practical problems in field research.* Hillsdale, NJ: Lawrence Erlbaum Associates.

Jussawalla, M., & Hughs, D. L. (1984). The information economy and indigenous communications. In G. Wang & W. Dissanayake (Eds.). *Continuity and change in communication systems: An Asian perspective* (pp. 251–266). Norwood, NJ: Ablex.

Karnard, B. (1987, May). Technology is new U.S.A. technology tool. *Financial Express* (New Delhi), p. 6.

Katz, E., Lewin, M. L., & Hamilton, H. (1963). Traditions of research on the diffusion of innovations, *American Sociological Review, 28,* 237–252.

Khalifallah, H. (1983, September). The Arab cassette culture. An underground response to censorship. *World Press Review, 30,* 38.

Kim, G. S. (1982). The new intellectual society. *Media Asia, 8,* 182–184.

Kurian, G. T. (1987). *Encyclopedia of the third world.* New York & Oxford: Facts on File.

Lent, J. A. (1988). India. In P. T. Rosen (Ed.), *International handbook of broadcasting systems* (pp. 133–145). New York: Greenwood Press.

Lent, J. A. (1986). New information technology: Myths, questions and alternatives. *Communicator, 21,* 392.

Libby, J. (1988). UNESCO and broadcasting research unit report. New York & Paris: UNESCO.

Lipset, S. M., & Solari, A. (Eds.). (1967). *Elites in Latin America.* New York: Oxford University Press.

MacBride, S. (1980). *Many voices, one world.* New York & Paris: UNESCO.

Mahan, E. (1985). Mexican broadcasting: Reassessing the industry-state relationship *Journal of Communication 35*(1), 60–75.

Mainwaring, S. (1987). Urban popular movements, identity, and democratization in Brazil. *Comparative Political Studies, 20,* 131–159.

Maitland, D. (1985). Independent commission for world-wide telecommunications development. *Telematics and informatics, 2,* 97–100.

Mallman, C. A. (1987, September). *Evolucion Y Revoluciones Societales* [Societal evolution and revolution]. Paper presented at the conference on Prospectiva Para La Formulacion De Politicas Y Estrategias En Ciencia y Technologia [Prospects for the formulation of policies and strategies in science and technology], Buenos Aires.

Mansfield, P. (1985). *The Arabs.* Ontario, Canada: Penguin Books.

Marker, J. (1987, August 14). Ambassador's message *Pakistan affairs, 40*(16), 1, 4–5.

Martin, J. (1981). *Telematic society: A challenge for tomorrow.* Englewood Cliffs, NJ: Prentice-Hall.

Mattelart, A., & Schmucler, H. (1985). *Communication and information technologies: Freedom of choice for Latin America?* Norwood, NJ: Ablex.

McDaniel, D. (1982). Libya. In D. A. Boyd (Ed.), *Broadcasting in the Arab world* (pp. 184–197). Philadelphia, PA: Temple University Press.

Middle East and North Africa, 35th ed. (1988). London: Europa Publications.

Mignone, E. F. (1987, September). *Educacion, Innovacion Technologia Y Prospectiva En La Argentina* [Education, technological innovation, and prospects in Argentina]. Paper presented at the conference on Prospectiva Para La Formulacion De Politicas Y Estrategias En Ciencia Y Technologia [Prospects for the formulation of policies and strategies in science and technology], Buenos Aires.

Miller, D. L. (1986). Mexico. In F. W. Rushing & C. G. Brown (Eds.), *National policies for developing high technology industries, international comparisons* (pp. 173–188). Boulder, CO: Westview Special Studies.

Montague, J. (1986, May). Congressional Committee Meeting Address, Washington, DC.

Mowlana, H. (1986). *Global information and world communication.* New York: Longman.

Mowlana, H. (1987, September). *Communication technologies and the Third World.* Paper presented at the conference Telecommunications and the Next Administration, Washington, DC.

Narula, U. (1984). *Dynamics of development communication: Awareness, motivation and participation.* Unpublished doctoral dissertation University of Massachusetts, Amherst, MA.

Narula, U. (1990). Grassroots movements in India. In I. Singh & J. Hanson (Eds.), *Advances in telematics* (Vol. 1, pp. 127–134). Norwood, NJ: Ablex.

National information technology plan (Singapore). (1985). In *Handbook of national development plans* (Vol. 2). London: Graham & Trotman.

NCT/NCT Newsletter (Vol. 1). (1986). Mexico City: Centro de Estudios sobre Cultura Transnacional.

Negroponte, J. D. (1986, May). Congressional Committee Meeting Address, Washington, DC.

Nyrop, R. F. (Ed.). (1978). *Iran: A country study* Washington, DC: American University.

Nyrop, R. F. (Ed.). (1984). *Pakistan: A country study* (5th ed.) Washington, DC: American University.

Nyrop, R. F. (Ed.). (1986). *The Yemens: country studies* (2nd ed.). Washington, DC: U.S. Government Printing Office.

Nyrop, R. F., Benderly, B. L., Conn, G. C., Cover, W. W., & Eglin, D. R. (1975). *Area handbook for Bangladesh, 1st ed.* Washington, DC: American University.

Nyrop, R. F., Benderly, B. L., Cort, A., Parker, N. B., Perlmutter, J. L., Shinn, R-S., & Shwanandan, M. (1982). *Sri Lanka: A country study.* Washington, DC: U.S. Government Printing Office.

Ogburn, W. (1927). *Social change with respect to culture and original nature.* Chicago: University of Chicago Press.

Pakistan facts and figures. (1987, August 16). *Pakistan affairs, 40*(16), 6.

Pakistan will accelerate the application of computer technology to development. (1986, May 16). *Pakistan affairs 39*(10), 4.

Pal, Y. (1984, April). Communicating the masses through satellite. *Communicator, 19,* 18–21.

Paz, O. (1983). *Tiempo nublado*. Barcelona: Sudamericana/Planeta.

Pitroda, S. (1987, April). *Telecom technology: A critical element for information systems*. Address at the seminar for Technology and Communication Development, New Delhi, India.

Rada, J. F. (1982). *The impact of microelectronics and information technology: Case studies in Latin America*. Geneva: UNESCO.

Revista De Derecho Espacial. [Magazine of space law]. (1986). Republica Argentina: Capital Federal.

Rogers, E. M. (1976a). Communication and development: The passing of the dominant paradigm In E. M. Rogers (Ed.), *Communication and development: critical perspectives* (pp. 121–148). Beverly Hills, CA: Sage.

Rogers, E. M. (1976b). New product adoption and diffusion. *Journal of consumer research, 2*, 290–299.

Rogers, E. M. (1986). *Communication technology: The new media in society*. New York: The Free Press.

Role of Adult Education and Mass Media for Civic Education. (1985, September). Report of the Asian Pacific Seminars, New Delhi, India.

Ropohl, G. (1983). A critique of technological determinism. In P. T. Durbin & F. Rapp (Eds.), *Philosophy and technology* (pp. 83–96). Dordrecht, Holland: D. Reidel.

Rosegger, G. (1976). Diffusion research in the industrial setting: Some conceptual clarifications. *Technological forecasting and social change, 9*, 401–410.

Saksena, K. P. (1986). *Cooperation in development: Problems and prospects for Indian and ASEA*. New Delhi: Sage.

Sarti, I. (1981). Communication and cultural dependency: A misconception. In E. McAnany, J. Schnitman, & N. Janus (Eds.), *Communication and social structure: Critical studies in mass media research* (pp. 317–344). New York: Praeger.

Saunders, R. J. (1986). *Telecommunications and economic development*. Washington, DC: World Bank Publications.

Schiller, H. (1983). Critical research in the information age. *Ferment in the field: Journal of Communication, 33*, 249–257.

Schnitman, J. A. (1984). *Film industries in Latin America: Dependency and development*. Norwood, NJ: Ablex.

Shramm, W., & Ruggles, W. L. (1967). How mass media systems grow. In D. Lerner & W. Schramm (Eds.), *Communication and change in the developing countries* (pp. 57–75). Honolulu: East-West Center Press.

Simpson Grinberg, M. (1986). Trends in alternative communication research in Latin America. In R. Atwood & E. G. McAnany (Eds.), *Communication and Latin American society: Trends in critical research 1960–1985* (pp. 160–172) Madison, WI.: University of Wisconsin Press.

Snow, P. G. (1985). Argentina. In H. Wiarda & H. F. Kline (Eds.), *Latin American politics and development* (2nd ed.). Boulder, CO: Westview Press.

Tehranian, M. (1988). Information technologies and world development. *Intermedia, 16*, 30–38.

Thongma, C. (1988, August). Telecommunications development in the asia pacific region in the last decade. *Asia Week*, pp. 22–25.

Tichenor, P. J., Olien, G. A., & Donohue, C. N. (1970). Mass media flow and the differential growth of knowledge. *Public Opinion Quarterly, 34*, 159–170.

Tigre, P. B. (1983). *Technology and competition in the Brazilian computer industry*. New York: St. Martin's Press.

Tuladhar, S. K. (1986). *Educational radio*. Unpublished manuscript, University of Massachusetts, Amherst, MA.

Umaseo, T. (1963, March). Joho Sangyo Ron [On Information industries]. *Chuokohron,* pp. 3–4.

UNCTAD–ESCAP. Regional seminar report. (1987, April), New Delhi, India.

UNESCO. (1970). *Science and technology in Asian development.* Switzerland: Author.

UNESCO. (1987a). *Statistical yearbook, 1987.* Paris: Author.

UNESCO. (1987b). *World communication report.* Paris: Author.

van Cuilenburg, J. J. (1987). The information society: Some trends and implications. *European Journal of Communication, 2,* 105–121.

Varis, T. (1984). The international flow of television programs. *Journal of Communication, 34*(1), 143–152.

Vizer, E. A. (1987, February). *La Crisis De Las Sociedades Nacionales Ante El Desafío De La Cultura Technologia* [The crisis of national society and the challenge of technological culture]. Paper presented to the Department of Information of the United Nations, "The Present International Economy of Service and Information, Changes in the Third World," New York.

Wang, G., & Dissanayake, W. (Eds.). (1984). *Continuity and change in communication systems: An Asian perspective.* Norwood, NJ: Ablex.

Weinstock, N. (1982, November–December). Smuggling television into Mexico. *Channels of Communication,* pp. 95–97.

Williams, R. (1983). *The year 2000.* New York: Pantheon.

Whitaker, D. P., Barth, H. A., Berman, S. M., Heimann, J. M., McDonald, J. E., Martindale, K. W., & Shinn, R-S. (1985). *Laos: A country study.* Washington, DC: American University.

World Bank. (1985). *Argentina: Economic memorandum* (Vol. 1). Washington, DC: Author.

Zuboff, S. (1988). *In the age of the smart machine: The future of work and power.* New York: Basic Books.

Author Index

Subject Index